Appropriating Folk Cultur

A Study of the Post-Independence Indian Drar

Appropriating Folk Culture

A Study of the Post-Independence Indian Drama

Guru Charan Behera

AUTHORSPRESS

Worldwide Circulation through Authorspress Global Network
First Published 2008
by
Authorspress
E-35/103, Jawahar Park
Laxmi Nagar, Delhi-110 092
e-mail: authorspress@yahoo.com

Appropriating Folk Culture: A Study of the Post-Independence Indian Drama
ISBN 978-81-7273-444-2

Printed in India at Tarun Offset, Delhi.

For my daughters

Pritipadma, Swetapadma and Shaswati

Preface

This book, comprising six chapters, discusses the use of the elements of folk culture in the plays of the Indian playwrights in the post-independence period. Some of the plays interpreted in this volume are in their original languages and others are in English translation. This has been indicated in the Select Bibliography. The plays in original are Asgar Bajahat's *Birgati* (Hindi), Sambhu Mitra's *Chand Banikar Pala*, Bibhas Chakrabortty's *Madhab Malanchhi Kahania*, Saonli Mitra's *Nathavati Anathabat* and *Katha Amruta Samana*, Sisir Das's *Bagh* (Bengali), Manoranjan Das's *Nandika Keshari*, Ramesh Prasad Panigrahi's *Mahanatak*, Karttik Chandra Rath's *Bahniman*, Niladri Bhushan Harichandan's *Kaluribenta*, Bijay Satpathy's *Ei je Surya Uen* (Oriya), Arun Sarma's *Buranjipat*, Satish Bhattacharya's *Maharaja* and Yugal Das's *Bayanar Khol* (Assamese). The quotations, from the plays in the original, used in the book, are translated into English by me. I hope to expand this book in future by including discussion on other plays and the plays in other Indian languages.

In this connection I express my gratitude to the Department of Culture, Government of India, for the award of Senior Fellowship in the field of literature and sub-field English for 2002-2004, which enabled me to write this book. I am obliged to the Department of Higher Education, Government of Orissa, for grant of two year study leave for the purpose.

During the period of my research many scholars in different regions have helped me in several ways. At Shillong and Guwahati I had fruitful interaction with Prof Birendra Nath Dutt, the then president of Assam Sahitya Sabha, Arun Sarma, a noted

Assamese dramatist, Ram Goswami, eminent Assamese folklorist, and Pradip Acharya, Reader in English, Cotton College, Guwahati, an Assamese critic and translator. I am grateful to all of them. My special thanks are to Arun Sarma for allowing me to have his interview. I express my gratitude to Dr. S.B. Medhi, I.A.S. (Retd.) for his help in facilitating these interactions during my stay at Guwahati.

I am grateful to Prof Debendra Raj Ankoor of National School of Drama, New Delhi, Prof K.Satchidanandan, former Secretary, Sahitya Akademi, Nirmala Kanti Bhattacharjee, former Editor, *Indian Literature*, H.S. Shiva Prakash of Jawaharlal Nehru University for their useful suggestions and references.

I am indebted to Late Prof C.D. Narasimhaiah and Prof C.N. Srinath for allowing me to use Dhvanyaloka library at Mysore. My gratitude is for Prof Chandrasekhar Kambar, an eminent Kannad poet, playwright and novelist for allowing me an interview. My thanks are for Dr Bijay Satpathy, Professor of Oriya, Utkal university and an eminent dramatist in Oriya for providing me some useful texts; for Bhanuti Devi, Reader in Assamese in the Eastern Language Centre, Bhubaneswar for helping me understand some Assamese texts, for Uma Sircar, Reader in Bengali, Ravenshaw University, Cuttack and Dr Subhra Prakash Das, Reader in English, Dhenkanal college, Dhenkanal for helping me understand the local and dialectical peculiarities of some Bengali texts.

I am thankful to the librarians and the staff of the libraries of National School of Drama, Sahitya Akademi, Sangeet Natak Akademi, Jawaharlal Nehru University, New Delhi; Harekrishna Mahtab State Library, Orissa and Ravenshaw College Library for their help and cooperation.

My thanks are for my students Prasant Sahoo, Manas Debata and Shiva Prasad Das of the J.N.U. for their help in locating certain research materials in New Delhi.

I thank my nephew Satyajit, daughters Pritipadma, Swetapadma and Shaswati for their help in the preparation of the manuscript. My thank is also for my wife Mina for taking upon herself much of the domestic burden and allowing me sufficient free time for the research work.

Guru Charan Behera

Contents

1

Folk Culture and the Post-Independence Indian Drama

The use of the elements of folk culture to express the contemporary Indian situation has become a significant aspect of Indian drama in various Indian languages after the independence. This has been as much a reaction against the hegemony of Western discourses as a search for our roots, our indigenous knowledge system, which westernised outlook has rejected as irrational and superstitious. The rich resources of folk culture, such as folk tales, songs, theatres, dances, rituals and even folk beliefs still kept alive by rural people and folk performers, and surviving as "traces" in cultural expressions in villages and cities, have opened up various alternative approaches for many modern Indian writers in their attempt to convey their sense of the world. This book *Exploring Folk Culture: Trends in Post-independence Indian Drama* based on this premise is an attempt to identify various folk forms variously used by the dramatists in Indian languages after the independence, and to study the rationale behind their use in general and in particular, the manner of their deployment, the effect of this deployment on the structures of the plays, and the complex network of interconnections among these plays, and so to make a broad comparative study.

The study seeks to prove the hypothesis that the use of folk elements in post-independence Indian drama is a part of the present-day socio-cultural programme of exploring the indigenous knowledge system to meet the present needs. Indian folk culture is a part of our indigenous knowledge system representing rural people's sense of mystery and wonder and the folk wisdom based upon their close and intimate perception of nature and society built up over the ages. Nowadays when we are turning more and more to our traditional beliefs and practices like those of yoga and ayurveda, various folk cultural forms and expressions invite the attention of artists and writers in search not only of new literary modes and techniques but also of answers to contemporary socio-cultural issues like social inequality in terms of class, caste and gender and corruption and exploitation. They try to relate the past to the contemporary sense of progress in a significant way, to reclaim the lost voices, revive the disappearing cultures and appropriate them for the present socio-cultural situation.

The methodology is cultural studies interdisciplinary, cross-cultural and comparative studies that seeks to combine the folklore studies with the literature and performance studies. As a study of the plays written in various regional languages in India, embodying various religious, ethnic and cultural voices, it seeks to bring in a multilingual and multicultural perspective, too.

Written Text as the Focus

I would like to make it clear in the very beginning that this study is based on the written texts, not on the performance pieces, of the plays for various reasons. First, in many Indian languages the highest place is given to the playwrights. The playwright is the initiator of the theatre and prepares the performable text. A theatre language of movement and gesture is meant to construct the text collectively not bypassing the model provided by the writer in his text. Second, play-scripts are easily available, whereas printed audiographic and photographic documentations of the production of important plays are rare. The photographs that exist are all posed, do not give any sense of continuity, real or imaginary. No photographs or sketches or sets and costumes, no recordings of voices and music can give us live and complete sense of performance. Set, music, costume and lighting designers however have not written or spoken about their works. Actors have not been able to articulate the principles underlying their performance. Third, there is the practical problem of seeing the theatre performances in far off places of India and understanding the regional languages of the performances.

I assume that all interpretative presentational possibilities exist simultaneously only in the written text, whereas specific production is reduction of those possibilities to a single interpretation, which is further reduced by the limitations of the group performers. So the published play is the chosen focus. But it does not mean the complete overlooking of the performance aspect, because performance carries the text to the stage and is a part of the extended text and needs to be studied as a dimension of the text. And since the folk theatre as a significant folk cultural form is performance-based how its performance aspects have been appropriated by modern playwrights is to be discussed. There are certain landmark plays remarkable for their use of folk elements available as performance scripts. They are the director's plays, in which case the director is the writer and producer. The bright examples, very relevant to this project are the theatres of Manipuri dramatists/directors Ratan Thiyam and Kanhailal, and even, of Malayalam playwright K.N. Panikkar.

A major problem one pursuing research in Indian drama faces the availability of texts is for many are out of print and many are difficult to locate as they remain scattered in far flung regions and locations difficult to negotiate. While studying written texts in various regional languages I have to depend mostly on translation. This is a major constraint, I think, not only for me but for all the scholars working on Indian literature. I am quite good at Oriya, my mother tongue, and English, my language of education and profession, but I can only read and speak Hindi and Bengali to a certain extent, and read Assamese. So far as other regional texts are concerned, I have to depend mainly on English translation. As I explore moving from place to place visiting libraries, corresponding with scholars and publishers I find many texts I have chosen for discussion have not been translated into any language known to me. So I have to deal with some original plays in Hindi, Bengali and Assamese, and in certain cases I have to take the help of people knowing these languages. For example, to understand Bibhas Chakrabarty's *Madhav Malanchhi Kahania* written in East Bengal dialect, I took the help of a lecturer in Bengali in my place.

This involves certain other problems which cannot be avoided. The study of certain plays in English translation and certain others in source languages may result in the unevenness or ununiformity in the study. Second, translation is an approximate representation of the original not its exact reproduction. Particularly the local peculiarities of many folk elements embedded in the texts are lost or glossed over in course of translation. Third, the difficulties in acquiring adequate practical knowledge about certain folk forms is an obstacle in comprehending the texts in their entirety. Fourth, the vast diversity of Indian culture and languages, diffusion of literary trends is simply bewildering. Hence the study is bound to be fragmentary and incomplete.

So far as the availability of the texts, and my knowledge of the regional languages are concerned I have chosen Hindi, Marathi, Bengali, Oriya, Assamese, Manipuri, Kannada and Malayalam plays, some in original and some in English translation, which have used folk elements, as the focus of my study. I have not included plays written in Indian English in the discussion because our Indian English drama expresses urban sophisticated life more than the folkways of life. I want to concentrate on *bhasha* literature and tradition. Among the varieties of the texts of multiple languages, races, cultures and regions, my attempt is to discover a network of multiple connections and differences.

Indian Literature: Indian Drama

The notion of Indian literature is yet to be concretised, given certain shape and significance to gain acceptability. Sisir Kumar Das in his essay "Construction of Indian Literature" writes that the nineteenth century Indologists, Albrecht Weber and Maurise Winternitz, implicitly created a "perception of Indian literature based on a pan-Indian language and that language was Sanskrit" (*New Comparison*, 1997 : 23). Edwin Arnold's *Indian Poetry* (1884) as an illustration of this perception included only excerpts from the *Mahabharata*, the *Hitopadesh* and the *Gitagovinda*. This gives an exclusive religious and philosophical colour to Indian literature and does not represent the Indian reality. Again, there are dangers of accepting a single language as a true vehicle of Indian literature, for it means absolute domination of one language and exclusion of other languages and people who speak them. This is a part of colonial enterprise of bulldozing India's diverse literary culture into following the western norm of selective marginalisation and delegitimisation of existing literatures and literary practices in various languages of regions and the constitution of an orientalist elitist version of classical Indian literary tradition.

There is a traditional notion that literature is entirely language based, and language as a cultural phenomenon is conditioned by its locale, and the socio-political forces that have been operating there. This does not adequately explain the concept of Indian literature because there is not a single Indian language. We may call Hindi literature, Tamil literature, Bengali literature but what is Indian literature? This argument also ignores the extra-linguistic civilisational elements—aesthetic, ethical, cultural, ethnic, and historical - that form the vital components of literature. So we talk of American Literature, Australian Literature, Canadian Literature, African Literature, etc., even though their language of expression is English, and even of Black American Literature, Hispanic Literature, etc. But Indian Literature, as such is a unique phenomenon, for it has both linguistic and extra-linguistic diversity. Regional, religious, ethnic, cultural variations add to the kinds of literature. Even in one language there are regional and diaelectical variations that lend further variety and peculiarity to Indian literature, for example, Bhojpuri, Maithili, etc., within Hindi literature. We should appreciate differences. As Aijaz Ahamad has stated multilingualism is the characteristic of Indian Literature. Multilinguality and polyglot fluidity operate, we find, in one geographical and civilisational space.

Many scholars, to explain the Indian literary situation, advance the concept of unity in diversity. Das insists that "there are enough unities underlying the differences in Indian languages that bring one nearer to the idea of an Indian literature" (24). Sujit Mukherjee appears to say, almost in the same vein, that any attempt to write a proper literary history of India (and not merely record the history of the literatures in various Indian languages) must proceed on the assumption that there is an Indian literature ("Towards a Literary History of India". *The Idea of an Indian Literature,* 1981 : 208-215). Once again Sisir Das in his monumental work *A History of Indian Literature1800-1910* and *A History of Indian Literature 1911-1956* emphasizes the unbroken continuity of the Indian literary tradition. But the reality is that there are bewildering varieties, differences, disagreements as to the geographical boundaries, the relation between castes and religious groups and the position of women. Das, here, talks in general terms when he talks of engagement with nation, world, geography, region and religion that can be applicable to all literatures in the world.

K.M. George in *Modern Indian Literature: An Anthology* quotes Nehru as saying that each of the Indian languages "is not merely the language of a part of India but is essentially a language of India, representing the thought and culture and development of this country in its manifold forms" (1992). George says that these words "point to the essential unity of our literatures without ignoring their diversities and distinctive features". When Nehru made the comment India had just got independence and the ravages of partition were fresh in the minds of Indians, and so his comment was the product of the crying need for unity and stability of the nation. But the political reality of present-day India strongly divided along caste, class, gender and ethnic and religious lines is different.

V.H. Gokak's definition of the Indianness of Indian literature as "living and dynamics awareness operating simultaneously at multiple points and levels" is rather rhetorical, not specific. C.D. Narsimhaiah in his collection of lectures *The Function of Criticism in India* locates Indianness in "the recognition of the spiritual behind the material in Indian life". This does not explain the works of the progressives, Urdu literature, Uttar-Adhunikata in literature, the Indian English novels which insist on the sheer materiality of existence, the Dalit writers who consider spirituality as a trap, and the works of Sadat Hasan Manto, Quarratulain Hyder, Eunice de Souza, et al. As Sarmistha Panja points out, these scholars "invariably fall back either on generalities that would be true of any literature, not just Indian, or they reduce the marvelous plurality of Indian literatures and unselfconsciously and hegemonically confine it within a single religious frame work" (*Many Indias* 2001: 6). How can we think of unity between the writing of a Brahmin writer from Hindi heartland and that of a Khasi writer?

So far as the place of English is concerned English cannot be excluded from Indian literary scene. U.R. Anantha Murthy admits that his mind is English, whereas his heart is Kannada and speaks of the " the Vedic mornings and Bernard Shaw evenings spent growing up in a village" ("On Being a Writer in India". *Tender Ironies*, 1994: 127–145). Noted critic Namvar Singh in "Decolonising the Indian Mind" (Trans Harish Trivedi, *Indian Literature, 1992*, 151) argues that Indian mind is not decolonised because the English speaking/writing elite demarcates Indian writing in English from Indian writing in regional languages. Though Salman Rushdie has contributed a lot in decolonising Indian writing by closely relating it to Indian culture, his remark that Indian English writing is far better than Indian regional literature betrays as much his ignorance about Indian literatures and Indian languages as the trace of colonial influence on him. Kapil Kapoor terms the colonial cultural hegemony as "metro criticism of metro – literature". "India was the data bank, the US supplied the theory" (Qtd. Panja, 7). Kapoor talks of Indian literature that excludes any thing that has to do with English. But it would be an act of historical falsification to erase the presence of English from Indian literature.

Kapoor's theorisation of "metrocriticism of metro literature" is relating to the westernised urbanised literature but does not take into account the writings of Premchand, Fakir Mohan, Gopinath Mohanty, Tarashankar Bandopadhyay, Bibhuti Bhusan Bandopadhyay, Mahasweta Devi and many other Indian writers, who have depicted rural tribal life and native tradition, and also the vast body of oral and folk forms which, as cultural expressions, belong to the family of literature. In such a situation there is the rise of bilingual, multilingual critics. More and more English literature people are turning to *bhashas* and are engaged in meaningful translation work or criticism and scholarship on Indian texts which may or may not have been translated. G.N. Devy in his *After Amnesia* (1992) postulates a theory of Indian

Bhasha Literature—that of the *desi* (native) uncontaminated by the *bidesi* (foreign) and the *Margi* (Sanskrit). He follows noted Marathi critic Bhalchandra Memade, who calls modern Indian literature as Anglo-*Bhatta* literature as it imitates English and Sanskrit traditions. One of the greatest losses during the Raj, according to Devy, is replacing of the reality of India's with a fantasy of the past, a false prioritisation of the West over the East as monolithic, superior, more rational and more powerful and the eclipsing of the regional languages, the *bhashas* in the formulation of Indian tradition in criticism.

The contribution of Nemade and Devy lies in the theorisation of the spaces, the *bhasha* traditions, from which resistances to the Western and elitist hegemony are to be carried out and of the programme of using our own indigenous knowledge system. But his pleading for a pure nativist Indian literary tradition smacks of cultural exclusiveness that goes against the basic concept of culture as something—dynamic living and growing-animating and appropriating other cultures.

Thus there are two basic premises of my study.

i) It tries to discover a network of interconnections and differences, not a single thread of unity, among Indian bhasha plays using folk elements. It skips too much insistence on unity, which it considers undefinable and elusive.

ii) There is a nativist thrust in the study but it does not altogether exclude the Western and Sanskritic elements. It is a creative alliance between various discourses. Even Brecht can be made to rub shoulders with our folk masters and our folk forms, we find, have also absorbed many elements of Sanskrit theatre.

What is needed is a creative alliance between cultures, an eclectically relevant appropriation of the elements of other cultures by a given culture, without letting itself be swept away. An attempt has been made in the directions by noted Bengali playwright-director Badal Sircar. Badal Sircar's concept of Third Theatre is an attempt at theorising such a synthesis between the city theatre having its base on Western theatre and the traditional village theatre:

> Today both theatres exist, each with its own strength and weakness, and it would be meaningless to select one and condemn the other. What we need to do is to analyse both the theatre forms to find the exact points of strength and weakness and their causes and that may give us the clue for an attempt to create a Theatre of Synthesis – a Third Theatre (*The Third Theatre*, 1983: 2)

POST-INDEPENDENCE

I have used the term "post-independence" but not the present-day much-talked about term, "postcolonial" mainly because it suggests the period after the independence of India, the dramas of which period are the subject of study. "Post-independence" is also a value-loaded term signifying the sense of freedom, joy and subsequent activities of reform and reconstruction and also the frustration and disillusionment that follows. The 'hyphen' here does not merely indicate temporal marker, it too indicates instant deconstruction, as it is used now a days in expressions like 'alter-native'/ 'de-scribe' /'re-place' etc. It means the aftermath of independence as well as the interrogation of our dependent past. Postcolonialism, on the other hand, is an ambiguous term, as it may refer to the time after colonialism has started, because the reaction against colonialism, it is argued, starts from the beginning of colonialism or to the time after colonialism is over. But post-independence is clear and unambiguous in referring to the period after the independence.

There is another confusion in the use of 'postcolonialism'. By common definition and usage as claimed by postcolonial theoriticians all postcolonial writings must be in English. And even the writers of *The Empire Writes Back* make idiosyncratic distinction between the "standard British English inherited from the empire and the english...in post-colonial countries", between the 'English' and 'englishes' (1987: 4). This hegemonic stance of such self-proclaimed anti-hegemonic discourse also rules out of it all the writing in the many Indian languages, which has in the past constituted the whole stuff and substance of Indian literature and which continues predominantly to do so even in post-colonial times. It is a strange argument that to merit the status of postcolonial literature a work of literature has to be written in English. Postcolonialism is a cultural situation, an approach. Language cannot be a determiner. Phaniswar Renu's *Maila Anchal*, Sri Lal's *Rag Darbari* (Hindi), Surendra Mohanty's *Andha Diganta* (Oriya) for instance no less effectively express postcolonial state. Harish Trivedi has stated:

> In the thousand year span and richness of its literary tradition, its thematic range and scope, and in sheer quantity as well as quality, Indian literature written in the modern Indian languages far outweighs Indian writing in English, which is seen to be currently grossly over-priviledged precisely because of its international 'post-colonial' connections. (*Critical Theory*, 1997 : 45)

There is an implied reference here to the claim of people like Salman Rushdie for the superiority of Indian writing in English.

Within the ambit of post-independence, I can say post-colonial issues can also be addressed. Postcolonialism has, no doubt, given centrality to the non-West in the Western discourse, and as a resistance to the Western hegemony it is useful to Indian society and culture and useful for my present project as it sets the indigenous against the Western. But within the anti-colonial culture there are elitist, Sanskritic, totalitarian nationalistic and even patriarchal forces that the marginalised faces, which postcolonialism cannot explain. The post-independence is the term then that can be used to address these various sets of opposition within the anticolonial, such as the totalitarian nationalist discourse/regional discourses, the Saskkritic elitist tradition (*Margi*)/the nativist *bhasha* tradition (*deshi*), the elite/the folk, the high caste/the low caste, men/women. India, to state the obvious, is a land of many religions, languages, and cultures, races and castes, which are cut through by class and gender factors. There are so many "imagined communities", to use Benedict Anderson's term, imagining their nations in their own ways. So the full implication of post-independence India is to be understood in terms of differences, vital diversity of Indian society. What is to be emphasized is the network of interconnections and differences between various literatures and discourses, interconnections at multiple levels that can explain the true spirit of unity in diversity. Hence in the use of various folk forms by writers in various languages this network of interconnections operate at multiple levels.

Folk Culture

Folk culture is the culture of the community specially belonging to rural areas – shared rituals and festivals, shared economic social customs, myths, fables and history. It evolved as accompaniment to and offshoot of various life functions, various phases of agricultural operation, hunting and trade that village people carried on. Songs, tales and performances expressed their joys, pain, wonder and mystery about their life and the world of nature. Many of them were meant to appease the forces of nature imagined by them as gods and goddesses. Folk culture, even though it becomes a deliberate social practice it retains its element of spontaneity. It is both participatory and spontaneous. Although never explicitly stated, the 'folk' is correlated to the tribal/village and group community, and 'classical' to the urban sophisticated, whether industrial or not. There have been a lot of exchanges between the folk and the classical.

In case of folk culture-performance individually the expression may be free, but in groups it is mostly a conditioned movement or sound directly related to life functions and experiences such as hunting, food gathering, agricultural activities connected with sowing, reaping and harvesting. Peasants engaged in agricultural operation devise many songs and dances of the propitiation of cosmic forces, of magic and sorcery. In course of time close to the village community but a class apart there emerged a group of professional singers, dancers, musicians, and actors, who are differently classified as Bhadas, Nats, Gandharvas, Vairagis, Binkaras, Yogis, etc. This is a group for whom the performance is a vocation, not a social, tribal or agricultural function. They move from place to place, have been responsible for the mobility of ideas, forms and styles between the villages and urban centers. "They have also been the vehicles of expression of protest, dissent and reforms, the carriers of reform movements and the articulators of satire and social comment and thus the instruments of socio-cultural change" (Kapila Vatsyayan, 1980 : 3). The contemporary forms such as *Bhavai, Nautanki, Terakooth, Veethinatakam, Ottandhullal, pala* etc., belong to this group. In artistic form, their technique ranges from acrobatic to pure spoken drama. The little village community has links not only with other little communities horizontally but with bigger life – worlds vertically through pilgrimage and religion, through trade and cultural influence.

Classical forms gradually evolved from folk forms. Vatsyayan has explained the evolution of classical forms as "[f]orms which developed within the framework of agricultural and other life functions and particular social organisations and carried forward and taken over in an urban milieu, though only after they have been dissociated from their original agricultural functions" (4). The intermingling of folk forms and city based classical forms has been constantly going on. So it is difficult to specify anything called folk forms. They all involve rigorous training under gurus that the classical forms possess as their feature. So the scholars like Nemichand Jain and Vatsyayan call folk theatres traditional theatres.

I have used the terms "folk culture" in the sense as it is commonly used. There may be classical elements in folk forms; the basic structure and framework remain folk-cultural. The term is used in a very comprehensive sense inclusive of folk tales, rituals, songs, dances, theatre, folk beliefs, etc. Certain Sanskritic Brahminic elements have been accepted, internalised and transformed by a community to give their folk forms a unique expressions peculiar to that community. For instance, we find many folk versions of Sutradhar of Natyashastra, in our folk performances. But at the same time it can be argued that the sutradhar might be a later version of the folk-narrator of the earliest of folk forms *uparupakas* that Bharat has indicated in his *Natyashastra*.

The Development of Indian Theatre

Folk forms definitely preceded theatre. Bharata in his *Natyashastra* refers to *uparupakas*, by which he might have meant the performances in villages. The dramatic lyrical pieces in *Rigveda* can also be the expressions of pre-existing folk forms. To protect the *uparupakas* disturbed by demons, obviously savage people, Bharat conceptualised the plan of theatre house. There was then a long and flourishing period of Sanskrit literature and theatre till the end of 10th century A.D. The folk forms continued at village levels, though many evolved into classical forms by being moved to urban areas and by acquiring certain sophistication. Both the forms affect each other all through not only vertically but also horizontally.

In villages the traditional folk theatre is a parallel stream that has been a part of the villagers life. Again there is professional folk theatre performed by professionals, who have formed communities and are identified as certain castes, as already stated. There are folk performances like Rama Lila, and Rasa Lila enacted by and participated by villagers. Later on particularly after independence attempts were made to combine the Eastern traditions—Sanskritic and folk and the Western traditions.

Here in this work my purpose is to work through the binary opposition of the classical form and the folk form and other related oppositions such as the elite and the folk, the *margi* (Sanskritic) and the *deshi* (regional literary tradition), the higher class/caste, and the lower class/caste, the nationalistic and the local, the Western and the Native, men and women, even the human and the non-human and to attempt to demolish the hierarchy between the two components of each set. The study begins with the assumption of the binary oppositions and moves on to deconstruct the hierarchy and thereby foreground and prioritise the second components such as the folk, the lower class/caste, the local, the native, women and even the non-human considered secondary and inferior in the traditional scheme of things. It seeks to reject, to use a Derridean perspective, anything called original and originary and the claim of superiority on the ground of purity. Classical forms are infected and influenced by folk forms and folk forms too by the former. Yet they are different from each other. Folk forms are distinguished by their performance conventions, setting and environment, actor-audience and actor-community interrelationship, common man's perspective, participatory performance mode, predominantlv oral tradition.

What is called "modern Indian theatre" can be traced to the second half of the nineteenth century in cities like Bombay, Madras and Calcutta, when English educated people started proscenium–stage tradition in imitation of the Western theatre. Before that Indian theatre was open-stage performance mainly based on religion and myth often presented as a ritual participated by the audience. The middle class people of these days wanted to behave and talk like English people to gain access to trade and administration controlled by the colonial power. The theatre imitated then the British theatre of the times presented by visiting troupes from England through the Proscenium stage or box-office structure. Stage with curtains representing walls from three sides and an invisible fourth wall between the stage and spectators represents a self-contained world to create the illusion in the minds of the audience that what they were seeing on the stage was reality or life. It was separated from the audience, there was no audience participation. Since financial investment was there and the spectators were to pay to see the theatre heavy doses of sentiment and entertainment were introduced. Earlier theatre had depended upon patronages of kings, ministers, local feudatories or temples. Actors had to improvise a lot to make it interesting and attractive because it presented myth-based stories familiar to the audience.

The philosophy of the proscenium theatre was secularism, aptly described by Girish Karnad as "commercially viable secularism" (Introduction", to *Three Plays*, 1999 : 25). As explained by Karnad it was partly necessitated by "the ethnic heterogeneity" of the new entrepreneurial class." In Bombay enterprises were financed by Parsis who spoke Gujarati. But the commonly understood language was Urdu popularised by Muslim rulers. Many of the writers employed by Parsi theatre were Muslims. The audience was largely Hindus. Karnad states:

> The consequences of this secularism were that every character on stage, whether a Hindu deity or a Muslim legendary hero, was alienated from his true religious or cultural moorings; and myths and legends, emptied of meaning, were reshaped into tightly constructed melodrama with thundering curtain lines and a searing climax. (25)

Troupes of professional actors called *natak* companies toured the countryside throughout the year and staged in semi-permanent structures on proscenium stages, with wings and drop curtains, illuminated by pefromax lamps. The regional theatres that came up in various languages in various provinces were all in imitation of the proscenium stage tradition.

The imitation of Western modes largely characterised Indian literature in 1950s and 1960s. Attempts were made to express local experiences and situations through Western modes, so to say to find native examples for Western modes. This became the nativisation of the Western and it gradually declined into the Westernisation of the native. For example, the absurd theatre movement, which was a powerful innovative dramatic mode used to express the post-World War situation of uncertainty and unpredictability in Europe, naturally captured the imagination of Indian dramatists of the post-independence post-partition era. But many dramatists used this absurd theatre mode with little regard for its relevance to the local reality, the present-day Indian situation. So we observe a gap between the reality of Indian life and the reality presented in these plays, between Indian culture and tradition and the culture and tradition represented in these plays. They became elitist and fashionable divorced from Indian life and culture. That triggered off reactions among the writers and moved them to relate Indian drama in a significant way to the social issues of our time and Indian culture. A further move in this direction in the 1970s was the attempt to relate Indian drama to the issues and situations faced by the common man of India, to the Indian culture participated by common man. So folk culture became a site for exploration. This is a part of the common man's perspective and the perspective of the marginalised. This coincided with the postmodernist project of the de-elitisation, the repudiation of meta-narrative as Francois Lyotard has interpreted. The focus shifted to the local, as Michel Foucault has urged the writers on little narratives, on minority literature to work. The use of the elements of folk culture in Indian drama is a movement in that direction.

Indian theatre is a very important example of the multilingual multi-cultural Indian literature. It is marked by a pluralistic experimentation with various prevailing trends in different parts of the country. Individual playwrights and directors with distinctive styles of their own share certain common contemporary social concerns that make them Indian at the core. In the 1960-70 period playwrights like Girish Karnad and Chandrasekhar Kambar from Karnataka, Badal Sircar and Mohit Chattopadhyay from Bengal, Manoranjan Das and Bijaya Mishra from Orissa, Vijay Tendulkar and Mahesh Elkunchwar from Maharashtra and Madhu Rye from Gujurat, writers, producers like Habib Tanvir from Chhatisgarh and Kanhailal Madhya Pradesh, Ratan Thiyam from Manipur, Utpal Dutt from Bengal, Shyamanand Jalan and Satyadev Dubey in the Hindi theatre, K.N. Panikkar from Kerala, Jabbar Patel and Sreeram Lagoo from Maharashtra and Pravin Joshi from Gujarat among many others are the real makers of the contemporary Indian theatre.

1960-70 period is a turning point in the history of the Indian theatre. Most of the above writers wrote some of their plays earlier but they began to attract public attention only after they were staged in 1960s. For instance, Dharamvir Bharati's (born in 1926) *Andha Yuga* written in 1954 came to be widely known and recognised as a powerful play only after it was staged in 1962 in Bombay directed by Satyadev Dubey. India fought two wars within three years with China in 1962 and Pakistan in 1965 with disastrous consequences on our economic growth. This period witnessed food scarcity in large parts of rural India, rural unrest exploding into armed uprisings of poor peasants under the Naxalite movement, industrial recession leading to retrenchment of workers, the organisation of dalits to articulate their demands for equal rights, aggressive assertion of rights by the downtrodden. Shaken up by this, sensitive writers and artists from the urban middle class milieu, turned their attention to the history and culture of the Indian lower orders, the landless peasants from the depressed castes, the dalit, the backward communities, the tribal people and their existential problems.

1960s marked the beginning of gradual collapse of certain values, norms and mores. Immoral practices in politics, horse-trading for formation of the government, use of money muscle power for buying votes, corruption in high places shocked middle class intellectuals. Deception, treachery and betrayal became the rules of life, unbelievably utter moral depravity, enormous gap between appearance and reality created a moral and spiritual void. It was against this background that in 1968 Habib Tanvir chose to stage *Mudrarakshasa*, a play written some 700 or 800 years ago by a Sanskrit dramatist called Visakhadatta. It was a period of experimentation with new ideas and styles influenced by contemporary trends in the West as well as the reinterpretation of indigenous traditions. The philosophy of existentialism, and the theatre of the absurd came as major influences for expression of the spiritual void, the prevailing state of uncertainity, unpredictability and disillusionment. Badal Sircar's *Evam Indrajit* is a major dramatic venture in this direction. The new generation of theatre practitioners were also beginning to rediscover their own mythology, their past history and folk cultural forms and use them on the stage in a style that struck a chord with the contemporary Indian audience.

Dharamvir Bharati's verse drama *Andha Yuga* in Hindi is one of the first such outstanding examples of such exploration of the Indian past. Mohan Rakesh's *Asadh Ka Ek Din*, an interpretation of the legend of Kalidas, is a play on the degrading limitations placed on the creative imagination of writers and artists. K.N. Panikkar directed and staged the plays of Sanskrit dramatist Bhasa, and in interpreting it from a modern perspective as a theatrical form he chose the traditional techniques of the Kodiyattam and the martial art of Kalari in Kerala. Both in content and form it is a creative fusion of the classical and the folk, the cosmopolitan and the regional, the past and the present. Girish Karnad's *Taghluq* is an interpretation of a historical character Md. Bin Tughlaq to reflect on the Nehruvian era in India. Utpal Dutt's *Tinar Talwar* expresses the theme of class differences through a presentation of nineteenth century Calcutta.

Folk Elements in the Post-independence Indian Drama

The exploitation of the folk culture for the resources relevant, in terms of theme and technique, to the contemporary situation is a part of the project of revisiting the past for the sake of the present. Brothers Grimm in Germany and the collectors of folk songs and ballads in England and in India had been inspired by a historical interest in the roots of a nation's culture and spiritual life. The idea had been to renew a nation's links with its past.

Folklore is always related to our literature as a constitutive part, or as scattered references, or as traces or invisible presences, because that forms our racial unconscious. An example can be given here of fourteenth century Oriya poet Sarala Das, who has used the resources of Oriya folklore for the reconstruction of an Orissan version of the *Mahabharata*. Typical folk rituals, sayings, anecdotes, riddles are used in it. The focus is on Bhima, not on Arjuna, and Bhima is an Oriya folk hero, a muscleman, wrestler or what we may call *pahalwan* trained in Oriya *Akhada ghara* (the dormitory for training in wrestling and bodybuilding). Shankardeva, the *Saint* poet of Assam, in his description of *Vaikuntha*, the abode of God Vishnu, in his work has turned to the wonderland of the folk tale and has given it a religious colouring.

The most remarkable example of the use of folk forms in twentieth century is Rabindra Nath Tagore's play *Rakta Karabi*. Actual and abstract allegorical beings like Jaggu Pahalwan and, Gosain and Raja, the embodiment of alienated humanity rub shoulders with each other without any sense of incongruity as in folk theatre. Tagore has not only lent the play a folk tale or fairy tale nature but also has used the folk form like the *boul*'s song (the wandering minstrel's song) in the play. Though industrialisation has brought about a disjunction between our present life and folk culture, we cannot make a complete sense of Indian literature without the knowledge of our folklore.

Theatre of Roots

After 1970 there have been conscious attempts to use the materials of folk culture in modern drama as a dramatic mode. It is called the theatre of roots movement. It is difficult to say who first started such an experiment because such movements came up in different places in different languages in different modes and styles. It may be almost at one time. Habib Tanvir, Girish Karnad,

Chandrasekhar Kambar, Vijay Tendulkar, Surendra Verma, Manoranjan Das and many others are pioneers in this direction.

In 1971 when Girish Karnad's *Hayavadana* (One with the Horse's Head) was published Dr. Suresh Awasthi, then secretary of Sangeet Natak Akademi-the National Academy of Music, Dance and Drama-in New Delhi commended *Hayavadana* as a sign of the emerging theatre of roots. He considered it as an example of what could be done creatively "with folk forms" in an urban setting, and credited Karnad with having evolved "a new dramatic form" (Qtd. Erin B. Mee, 2006:145). It was for him "an indigenous nonrealistic style of production" which in turn could be used to define "Indian theatre" (1989:50). The term 'indigenous' as it is use in the discussion of the roots movement refers to performance genres that were fully developed and established in the pre-colonial era and have been supposedly unaffected by the impact of colonialism. B.V. Karanth's 1972 production of the play in Delhi, "according to him reversed the colonial course of contemporary theatre" (*TDR* 1989:48).

The theatre of Roots was a part of larger project of decolonisation that has taken place in the nation as a whole. The idea of modern theatre in India largely influenced by the western plays and mainly associated with English- educated urban club was in direct contract to indigenous popular entertainment, ritual performance, and plays with mythological subjects associated with lower classes. The divide was created between English/urban theatre and Indian/rural performances. The performances that depended up on what is called archival knowledge (playscripts) were thought of as high culture and performances depending on embodied knowledge (embodied in memory-repertoire of gesture, tone of voice, movement, music) as low culture. So in 1970s and 1980s there started the roots movement as medium of resistance to colonial theatre and colonial attitude toward theatre. Hebib Tanvir known as a director for his pioneering use of popular performance style in theatre production felt in the same way that two hundred years of "alien rule had destroyed India's cultural identity". It brought about what G.N. Devy calls cultural amnesia', which is to be fought against. Tanvir called for 'our own plays about our own problems in our own forms" (*Theatre Journal* 1981:59).

But there is the apprehension of the theatre of roots movement ending up in what Partha Chatterjee calls a "framework of false essentialism" (*Thought and* ....1989:134). Chatterjee shows how the discourse of nationalism in nineteenth century India contained an inherent contradiction, for it challenged the colonial claim to political domination while accepting the "intellectual premises of modernity' on which colonial domination was based" (30). Modern drama thus is basically a hybrid form and if we forget and ignore this there is the possibility of being trapped in the "framework of false Indian essentialisms".

Modern Indian Drama as a Hybrid

The post-independence plays that turn to the folk culture for their source and support have to appropriate, undermine, and adopt and redirect elements and attitudes of the colonial culture to create space for and foreground the folk elements and forms. Appropriation, in this content means the deployment of anti-illusionistic modes as evolved by Lugi Pirandello, Betrold Brecht, Antonin Artaud, Jerzy Grotowski, Joseph Chaikin and others to suit the contexts different from their 'original' ones, and, I may say, in the service of the emerging Indian dramaturgy based on folk culture. This notion of 'original' gets deconstruted too as these theoreticians have based their theories on the oriental theatre. For instance Artaud admitted that his Theatre of Cuelty was inspired by the oriental theatre-particularly Balinese theatre. These folk-form-based plays undermine the illusionist naturalist conventions and adapt, not adopt, the relevant parts of western discourse-all these for their folk culture mode. Western theories have sensitised our playwrights to the enormous dramatic potentialities of Indian folk forms and in that sense, too, are relevant for our dramatists.

There is a lot of parallels we find between the European experimental dramatic devices and Indian folk-forms. I would like to begin with Italian dramatist Lugi Pirandello's metathetrical mode inaugurated in his path-breaking play *Six Characters in Search of an Author* (1921). It is based upon the notion that the play can be the subject of the play and that there are only masks which hide the face and roles that conceal the elusive suffering individual. It refers to the structure of the play-within-the-play or the play-about the play. This can be the precursor of the metafictional mode or the self-referential, self-conscious scheme of writing that the present-day postmodernism advocates. Indian folk-narrative tradition of the string of tales, or the frame-story, the story within the story, the story branching out of the story-parallels this Pirandellian structure.

Betrold Brecht's concept of epic theatre is a mode of subversion of the invisible fourth wall between the stage and the audience, which is akin to the denial of any boundary between the performance and the audience in our folk performances. This is evident at a much larger scale in community theatres like *Ramlila* and *Krishnalila*. An example of this is or Ramnagar *Ramlila,* in which case entire Ram Nagar and Varanasi turn into a stage. Another example is that of *Dhanu Yatra* in Baragarh in Sambalpur district of Orissa. During the nine-day yatra the river called *Jira* becomes Yamuna and Amapalli village on one side of the river becomes mythical Gopapur and Baragarh town on the other side becomes Mathura. Starting from the birth of Krishna till the death of demon king Kansa all the episodes are enacted in different places of Amapali and Baragarh. Apart from trained actors playing various roles the people of Amapali and Baragarh play *gopalas* (milkmen) and *gopis* (milk-women) and the citizens of Mathura. It is a festival in which people of the entire area participate. And during these days Kansa becomes the absolute ruler, who, according to the custom is not only obeyed by the people of Baragarh (representing Mathura) but also by government officials. The actor playing Kansa speaks a mixture of stylised and colloquial dialogues of words and expressions from Sanskrit, Oriya, Hindi, English etc, and even comments on the contemporary social, political and economic situations. This separates the actor from the character which Brecht has advocated as a device of alienation effect. Richard Schechner an eminent theatre theoretician and director has formulated his 'environmental theatre' based on his study of Ramnagar Ramlila. Here the aesthetic, social, religious and mystic coalesce, played out in an actual physical space. Schechner has stated:

> And it is precisely this kind of meta-aesthetic sense-an aesthetic that goes beyond aesthetics-that western conte.nporary theory lacks. (1983:302)

Brecht, Artaud and Schechner work towards a participatory theatre, which Indians have been performing as ritual.

This concept of the theatre as ritual the basis of Antonin Artaud's Theatre of Cruelty. He calls his theatre as the theatre of metaphysics that enfronts the spectator with himself, with the cosmic wonder and mystery. It is the externalisation of a depth of latent cruelty. It was a theatre of cestasy meant to induce a trance like state in the audience. His theories, he admitted, were based on the oriental theatre where he found his answer to the problem of theatrical language "half way between gesture and thought" (*The Theatre of Cruelty* 1968:55). The emphasis was on the nonverbal. He brought the magical to the stage, conceived characters as *shaman*—the magician-priestly figure of the primitive practices that we find in our folk ritual theatres and tribal culture. Jerzi Grotowski developed this Artaudian model of the physicalisation of abstractions to develop his 'poor theatre' which can be defined as the theatre of minimalism—bare stage, emphasis on the non-verbal, physicalisation of emotion and abstraction through physical gestures and configuration, exploitation of sounds like grunt, groan, scream and chants. This was adopted by the Living Theatre and the Open Theatre of America in 1960s. Joseph Chaikin, the exponent of the Open Theatre used the transformation technique, according to which an actor has to play different roles and an actor through poses and gestures or actors through body-formation represents various emotions, situations, scenes and even objects. An actor, through various transformations and role-playings represents a charcter not as a single fixed identity, but as a compound of multiple identities. It is to subvert any kind of fixity to its identity. Manipuri playwrights Ratan Thiyam and Kanhailal, Malayalam playwright K.N. Paniker practise ritual or liturgical theatre that Artaud advocated and folk performers of India practise. They make the actors undergo rigorous physical training as grotowsky does in his polish Theatre Laboratory. Thiyam and Kanhailal use Manipuri martial art tradition to dramatise their sense of the present time.

So Indian playwrights locate the transformation mode in their own folk forms, for instance Saonli Mitra discovers it in plenty in Bengali pala and Maharashtrian *Pandavani*, Utpal Dutt in Palla. In them the chief singer *Gayaka* and the supporting singers *Judi* or *palia* while narrating and singing mythological tales act out differ mythological characters through changing gestures, movements, voice-modulation and slight modification of their costume and through improvisation. In Mitra's *Nathabati Anathabati* only two singers act out the roles of Draupadi, Kunki, Arjun, Bhima and others. This achieves the required alienation effect as, actors are not completely identified with roles and the audience feels that this is 'acting' not 'reality'.

Folk Forms as the Dominant

What the playwrights under discussion do is to blend the folk forms and elements with relevant and related western modes and devices. They are made interrelated and are used for functional purposes. But while folk elements are foregrounded others are backgrounded purposes, if we use the formalist theory to explain the point. Here I can use Roman Jakobson's concept of the dominant to explain the position of Indian folk elements in relation to other elements or devices in such plays. Writing in 1935 Jakobson defined the dominant as "the focusing component of a work of art: it rules, determines and transforms the remaining components" (Qtd. Selden, 1989:15). The dominant provides the work with its focus of crystalisation and facilitates its unity or gestalt (total order). Literary works for Jakabsen are dynamic systems. In the plays to be discussed in this book the folk elements function as the dominant, the focusing component that assimilates and controls other devices like those of metatheatre epic theatre, theatre of cruelty etc. These plays thus it can be said, foreground the folk, the local and background the classical and the elite.

There are various ways of using folk forms in modern drama. An existing folk play can be interpreted as a comment on the present situation. A play can be an imaginary folktale invented and developed by the dramatist. Folk theatre styles like those of *Yakshagana, Yatra, Pala, Tamasa* are used in the perfomance of the plays. Even though there is no explicit use of any folk form, some plays are staged in folk performance style as in the case of Habib Tanvir's production of *Mrichha Katikam* The use of folk elements, I can point out, thus establishes the living connection with our tradition, gives the work of art order and clarity of expression. It is a reflection upon the contemporary situation and sometimes functions as a critique on social inequality and moral depravity in the present times.

2

Post-Independence Hindi and Marathi Drama Experiment in Folk Forms

HINDI DRAMA

It is Dharmavir Bharati's *Andha Yuga*, which set the trend in the use of the past resources for reflection on the contemporary situation. The mood of disillusionment, chaos and confusion, dilemma and ambivalence that characterised the post-Nehruvian era was dramatised through the myth of the Mahabharata war and its aftermath. Then Mohan Rakesh in his *Asadh Ka Ek Din* (*One Day in Ashadha*) reconstructed the legend of Kalidas to present his critique of the state control, explicit or implicit, through censorship or officiation that hampers creative activity. Bhisam Sahani's *Madhav*i used the myth of Madhavi to castigate the increasing commodification of women in our times. The exploration of folklore as a part of the programme of revisiting the past has then become a part of the dramatic mode in certain plays of Hindi playwrights like Habib Tanvir, Surendra Verma, Asgar Bajahat, Marathi playwrights like Vijay Tendulkar and Satish Alekar.

HABIB TANVIR'S *CHARANDAS CHOR*

Habib Tanvir's *Charandas Chor* (1975) is a landmark text known for the full exploitation of folk culture elements. Tanvir's interest in the folk dates back to his IPTA (Indian People's Theatre Association) days in Bombay during the 1940s. As a child he had often visited villages and listened to the music and songs of the local folk, was fascinated by their enchanting melodies. His exposure to the use of traditional forms like the *burakatha* and *powra* used in the works of Hindi, Gujarati, Marathi and Konkani writers during his IPTA days rekindled his interest in folk culture. Later on he returned to that folk music and began to collect Chhatisgarhi folk songs.

In 1954 Tanvir moved to Delhi, where he wrote and produced *Agra Bazaar,* his first major stage production. The play is based on the work and times of a very unconventional eighteenth century Urdu poet Nazir Akbarabadi, who not only wrote about ordinary people and their everyday concerns but wrote in a style and idiom, which was a radical departure from the orthodox, elitist norms of decorum in poetic expression and subject matter. Tanvir, like Akbarabadi offered an experience radically different both in form and context from anything that fashionable Westernised theatre could offer.

Tanvir had his training in theatre in England at the Royal Academy of Dramatic Arts and Bristol Old Vic Theatre School. He travelled extensively through Europe and watched a lot of theatre. Disregarding the colonial mindset that dominated the contemporary theatre scene at the time, he began his long quest for an indigenous performance idiom. That led him to the folk performance modes and folk artists. The first production of his *Mitti Ki Gadi* a translation of Sudraka's *Mrichha-Katikam* included six folk actors from Chhatisgarh. His theatre derives its inspiration, its actors, its techniques, stage construction and often plots from the folk tradition. His involvement with the folk is motivated mainly by two reasons. First, he is aware of the creative possibilities and artistic energies inherent in various folk forms, their continuing social vitality in rural India despite serious erosion and debasement in the wake of ruthless urbanisation and homogenisation through cinema and TV. He says,

> I was not running after folk forms, I was running after folk actors. There is a big difference here because when I used the folk actors, they brought the folk forms with them. I did not have to academically impose upon them. And I did not really think a lot about the forms as such, I was freely using

> imagination to interpret a play and these actors had the forms. So to that extent, in that subtle and indirect manner, their forms come. But, in another sense, none of these forms are represented in my production. (Qtd. Javed Malick, "Introduction", *Charandas Chor* XVIII)

The performance style of his actors is, no doubt, rooted in their *nacha* background but his plays are not, I can point out, exactly *nacha* production. He has even used folk style to stage classical plays like *Mudrarakshas* bringing about a blending between the two. This brings us to the second reason. He does not romanticise the folk uncritically or ahistorically. Aware of their historical and cognitive importance he allows his own modern consciousness and political understanding to interact with the traditional energies and skills of his performers. He works to achieve the sense of socio-political immediacy and artistic sophistication without losing any of the very beauty and simplicity of folk performance.

Javed Malick has traced the genesis of *Charandas Chor*:

> *Charandas Chor* had a long and interesting genesis, involving a protracted process (about two years) of experimentation and improvisation before it reached its final shape in 1975. Briefly, Tanvir first heard the story in 1973 from the folklorist Vijayadan Detha – who had, in turn, recorded it from the oral cultural tradition of Rajasthan. Later that year, Tanvir tried to use the story during a *Khayal* workshop in Rajasthan. But it did not work. Some time later, he held a month-long workshop with several *nacha* groups in Bhilai, towards the end of which he made his actors do an improvisation on the Rajasthani folktale about a thief. A rough shape emerged from the exercise. Tanvir presented the far from finished attempt at an all-night function of the Satnamis (a religious sect) in the open air Bhilai maidan incorporating into it a number of panthi songs and instantly improvising some others. ("Introduction" – XIII)

Charandas Chor is a tale of the rise of a petty village thief to the status of a popular hero. The real protagonist of this play like his other plays is the ordinary people. Charandas represents a common man capable of virtues rare in an unjust class-based society.

The play opens with a *panthi* song sung by a group of *panthi* dancers, dancers and singers, of the Satnami sect, who are the followers of Guru Ghasidas. This *panthi* folksong proclaims that the truth is divine, the divine is the truth. This sets the mood and framework of the play that presents Charandas's persistent effort in not telling lies, that leads him to death. He is a professional thief superior to many other non-professional thieves who indulge in corruption, misappropriation and looting of public money and taking bribe:

> There are so many rogues about, who do not look like thieves,
> Impressive turbans in their heads softly shod their feet,
> But open up their safes and you will surely see,
> Stolen goods,ill-gotten wealth, riches got for free.
>
> (*Charandas Chor*, 24)

A sense of collective community is also conveyed through the chorus suggesting the need for reviving the community spirit that is on the wane. After the song Charandas enters with a heavy bundle of clothes on his back singing a song likened to children's rhyme. This is about the cat looking for mice, who gather around her and dare to tickle her, which is interwoven into the play here and there. The motif of the cat chasing the mice and the mice playing tricks with the cat is a folk motif related to Charandas stealing the golden *thali* and constantly hoodwinking the havildar in search of him. Charandas is more and more thrilled by the success of his tricks, his act of thievery, particularly in robbing the people considered mighty and witty in the society. He is more in love with his art than with the end, more with his cunning way of getting wealth than with the possession of the wealth. He reduces human beings to counters in his game. By trapping people through his tricks he mercilessly exposes man's vulnerability to greed and hypocricy. His is like Ben Jonson's Votpone. He does not like to deceive poor and innocent people. That is proved when he dupes a woman but finding her weep he becomes sympathetic and returns her jewellery, and when he helps the peasant, whom he has once robbed.

Guru, in the play, is a common man's guru; though he has pecuniary interest he has reformed many people, made them give up drinking, gambling and stealing. Charandas vows before the Guru that he won't eat off a golden plate, will never mount an elephant and lead a procession, will not even marry a queen and be a king and will not tell lies. These are the things which he has not expected at all to come his way. Ironically all these come his way.

Charandas very cunningly robs the greedy exploiter landlord of his sacks of rice in spite of his guards and securities, and distributes them among the poor. He then helps the peasant, whom he has once robbed. These acts of exploits, cunningness and generosity make him a popular hero. In Scene 4 the *panthic* chorus sings.

> Oh listen, brothers and sisters, to what we have to say,
> Charandas is not a thief, a thief, no way. (p. 26)

The landlord, the priest and the munim are contrasts to Chandras. The former are apparently honest but really thieves, the latter is apparently a thief but really honest. He robs those who rob people, common men. The havildar mistakes the landlord as the thief and this mistaken identification, though comical, points to the truth that the landlord appears to be honest but is really a thief. Charandas also plays tricks on the priest of the temple. He first gives him jewellery as offerings for the deity, spends the night with him in the temple, massages his legs, wins his trust and then in the darkness of the night steals all the ornaments of the deity and the idol. This act of Charandas is an indictment of the way religion is being used for acquiring wealth and power. The scene ends with a *panthic* song that comments on the present day situation:

> The thief is a king, the king is a thief,
> The gods and the thieves, they dance cheek to cheek,
> The doctors themselves are too sick to take care,
> Oh, here comes the thief, out of the air. (29)

The ubiquitous thief is like a god, who is used by priests and the rich for commercial gain. This is questioned by Charandas's radically subversive act.

The last robbery that Charandas commits is the robbery of royal treasure just to show that he can hoodwink and deceive the strongest of royal security guards. In the guise of a minister he comes for inspection, takes away only five gold mohurs. When the munim finds that five gold mohurs are missing he takes out another five and declares that ten are missing. But in the court he shows the five gold mohurs he has stolen and exposes munim before the queen. This exposes the corruption in administration, bureaucracy and in temples and religious organisations. He says,

> Others steal in the sly, while I do it in broad day light with great fanfare.
> That's the only difference. (37)

The queen gets attracted towards this thief for his honesty and his forthrightness, his energy and vitality. He refuses to eat off the golden plate delicacies offered by the queen, ride elephant to lead the procession to be accorded honour by the queen, turns down the approach of the queen to marry her and become the king. Then the queen asks him not to reveal to others her request for marriage but he reminds her of his vow he has made before his guru not to tell lies. That leads to his punishment and his death.

Charandas Chor is a subversive text that uses folk elements to subvert the ideology of corrupt elitist people in power. Queen's fascination for him is a commentary on female sexuality. His unorthodox, deviant attitude, his gusto and vitality, his commitment to what he thinks right might have attracted a lady leading a highly formal cloistered life and trying to come out to the open outward world. This also marks what Bakhtin calls "grotesque" – the lowering down of the high, of the elitist. (*Problems of Dostoevstg's Poetics* 122). Cut off from reality, from the earthy, the vital by high royalty, high religion, high formality and sophistication her sexuality has been atrophied. The sheer force of crude but honest vitality of Charandas arouses her sexuality. His commitment to truth is a form of discipline, with which he tries to contain his energies, give them some shape and form. His vow not to tell lies questions and highlights falsity, hypocricy, and affectaton in society. Here the official authority, the authority of the queen marked by pompous outward show, corruption, looting of public treasury comes in conflict with the authority of the truth. Inspired by Charandas the queen in the beginning takes action against corruption, but her frustrated sexuality and the challenge to her authority by the commitment to truth and her fear of being exposed, later on, takes a vengeful form.

Charandas dies a martyr to the truth, a true inheritor of Guru Ghasidas's legacy. Performed in *nacha* style by real *nacha* folk actors of Chhatisgarh the play presents the perspective of the common man, of marginalised people. *Nacha* form is full of songs and dances and even acrobatics performed by trained actors. It is like a carnival, as Bakhtin has pointed out, in which social hierarchy is denied, everything is topsy-turved. The explosive humour and comedy which is a part of our folk culture tradition is used to ridicule the corruption and hypocrisy in our state. The characterisation of Charandas is, thus, an attack on the social hierarchy that legitimises social inequality.

Surendra Verma's *From Sunset to Sunrise*

Surendra Verma's *From Sunset to Sunrise* is a reworking of a folktale to critique the patriarchal tradition that reduces woman to an object and to a breeding machine. The tradition of *Dharmanati* requires that the queen, if she is not able to produce any heir to the throne, has to come out in a ceremonial way to seek a man outside the palace in order to conceive. This is used here as a symbol of high class/caste patriarchy and the queen in the play uses this tradition to subvert this tradition itself.

The queen was from a poor family and was in love with a poor young man. But she had to marry king, Okkak, the king of Malla, for her family's desire for upward mobility in socio-economic ladder and also as a submission to the oppressive feudal patriarchal system. She had to marry the king because his horoscope matched with hers. The fact that the king's horoscope matched with hers alone is an evidence of the way religion is used by the dominant for perpetuation of their domination over the marginalised. Many years after their marriage they have no issue and the king has been ailing for more than a month. According to the custom as soon as five years of a marriage is completed, an announcement regarding a successor to the throne is to be made.

If that is not possible the custom of *Niyogi* is provided not only in Malla but also in the neighbouring kingdoms like Kundanpur and Avanti. The queen will have to become *Dharmanati*. Anguttara Nikaya, the royal priest, justifies this practice of making love on the part of the queens to persons other than their husbands, for continuance of the dynasty and for the preservation of the kingdom. In the *Mahabharata* Kunti and Madri have to resort to this method because Pandu is barred by curse from any sexual relationship. The impotence and weakness of the king has made Malla vulnerable to internal disturbances and external attacks. And the impotence of the king is itself symptomatic of the moral and spiritual decay.

Here the individual is pitted against the system. Ministers and advisers rule out the king's protest against this. Very ironically here a woman is to be punished for the weakness of a man. Sheelvati, the queen says:

> They (your poets) call me, 'The one untouched by the rays of the sun'... And tonight, the same woman will walk into the Palace courtyard, with the Jaimala in her hands, the centre of attraction of thousands of pairs of eyes... And will walk away with some man for this one night... (*Modern Indian Drama* 396).

Asuryampashya (one untouched by the sun) and *Dharmanati* are two opposite patriarchal constructions – one to keep woman confined to home, the other to turn woman into a legalised prostitute ignoring her wishes and desires. In her marriage to Okkak, Sheelvati has no choice of her own, she has been chosen by the king. She has to abandon her lover because he is poor. She has not got any sexual satisfaction from her marriage with the weak impotent king. She will have to offer herself to an absolutely strange man outside her wedlock. The issue, who will be born outside the wedlock, will be very ironically crowned as the prince and subsequently as the king. That poses the existential question of the parentage. What has been conventionally regarded as immoral is legitimated by tradition, by the collective desire appropriated by the council of ministers.

Mahattarika, the king's female attendant, relays to the king the situation of the queen proceeding with the garland in hands among the persons waiting in a line and offering it at the end to Arya Pratosh, well known businessman of the town. That man, it is found, was once that lover of Sheelvati, who was abandoned because he was poor at that time.

Act two presents two parallel episodes, which are shown alternatively. The king asks Mahattarika to tell him from her own experience the mystery and pleasure of sexuality—when she and her husband have sex, when they enjoy it most, whether Sunday is the day of greatest sexual enjoyment. This expresses his awareness of his impotence and his feeling of restlessness, inferiority when his wife is courting another man. This is counter-pointed by the scene between Sheelvati and her present paramour Pratosh. Sheelvati tells him how she turned into a *Bishakanya* (Maiden of Poison) because of the doses of bitterness and frustration injected into her by poverty before her marriage; though after the marriage bitterness is gone she has remained a virgin (being married to an impotent); hunger is gone but the sexual hunger remains. This contrapuntal structure of the scene illustrates the juxtaposition of warm fulfilling love between Pratosh and Sheelvati, and disillusionment and frustration in the intimacy between Okkak and Mahattarika, when Okkak feels aroused but is not capable of fulfillment. He confesses:

> No young woman on this earth has anything to fear from me...(419)

He married Sheelvati, because his horoscope had not matched with that of any other woman and the royal physician had told him that marriage would cure him of his lack of sexual excitement. Sheelvati was a poor girl who got wealth through the marriage but now she gets love ironically in playing *Dharmanati*, making love outside marital relationship. She uses the tradition of *Dharmanati* a patriarchal design for her fulfilment that eventually goes against the patriarchal authority.

Sheelvati has waken up to the wonders of the body, mystery of the sex. Earlier, days after days she has felt hot and tormented within, tried all means to cool her passion and her urge but has failed and become furious with everybody and everything:

> ... but let me tell you that following the norms of married life for five long years has not given me the kind of satisfaction that I have derived from one night alone... The molten lava buried deep inside me for years burst into flames, the moment he touches me ...(416)

The very dichotomy between the body and the mind is dissolved here. The traditional neglect of the body and prioritisation of the soul over the body is refuted here. She revolts against the institution of marriage, even the institution of the state, all codes and norms that try to stifle individuality, turn woman into a breeding animal, and control and manipulate the human body.

> But now, I no longer want to live my life according to books
> ..Now I want to live life, as it really is. (418)

When she is told that she has to conceive, become a mother, give an heir to the throne she rejects this notion:

> ..the ultimate fulfillment of womanhood is not in motherhood, Prime Minister! Her actual fulfillment is in this, this satisfaction that she derives from her physical union with man and motherhood is only a secondary byproduct of the fusion. (418)
>
> ..butter is what you get when curd is churned, but you also get buttermilk as a residual secondary product ...(to all those present) we are also like butter milk ...the butter that enriched out parents' lives was something else ...(To Okkak) What are you? Only a symbol of that nocturnal partnership, a public announcement of those confidential and intimate moments shared by your parents ...a visible supplement of their personal, invisible history which later got added on to the original book – whether the creator wanted it or not ..(419)

She tells the Prime Minister and others that last night her paramour gave her a contraceptive medicine, again she will take it and there is no chance of her becoming mother. Again she will appear before the public as a *Dharmanati.* Okkak's comment ironically sums up the transformation of the queen: "The queen had gone out as a *Dharmanati* and has returned as a *Kaamnati*" (421). He used her in the beginning as a drug to arouse himself, cure himself of his sexual deficiency. The state has tried to use her as a state property, a commodity. She has so far played being for others, being for him the king, and for the subjects. Now she searches for being-for-herself, for an authentic existence.

Underlying this existential theme is the factor of gender. Sheelvati rises against feudal patriarchy that reduces woman to a slave, an object with no wishes and desires, a play in the hands of the males. Here very ironically Sheelvati uses tradition to subvert the constrictive forces of tradition. She accepts the custom of *Dharmanati* and goes public to choose her paramour but uses this opportunity to satisfy her deepest longing, and to have fulfilment in life. If extramarital sex is granted by society through the custom of *Dharmanati*, why should not a woman who is forced into marriage to an impotent be allowed to go for extramarital relationship? The woman here revolts against the institutions of marriage and state authority that stifles individualism, and regulates the body. She takes possession of her body and saves it from the degradation it has been subjected to by the feudal patriarchal order. She restores it its dignity and uses it for her love and deeper satisfaction. It is from the body that she fights the patriarchy.

Asgar Bajahat's *Birgati*

Asgar Bajahat's *Birgati* has used the elements of *nautanki*, a folk theatre form of Uttar Pradesh to critique the money-power nexus that smothers any revolt in the contemporary society. In *nautanki* style dialogues are rhetorical punctuated by plenty of songs and dances. The characters often speak in songs to express their intensity of emotion. Songs are made dramatic by being put in the form of duet or of response and counter response. Humorous interludes are used to lighten the atmosphere. This folk mode gives a folk perspective to the entire situation and presents it from the common man's viewpoint.

The story is in the form of a folk tale. It is an allegory of modern life marked by excessive materialism, decline in moral values, glaring social inequality, and the perversion of aesthetic sense. Sukumar, the only child of five brothers, the richest Sahukars in the town is a sensitive young man who is nauseated with the world of materialism, and does not take any interest in the worldly affairs and their business empire. He is shocked to see the inequality among people-while some indulge in excess of luxury, some starve. He is a poet at heart, meditates on the wonders of nature. The play opens with poetic evocation of the beauty of nature, the patches of cloud floating in the sky, the cool wind, the Koel's song, Papihe's melody and the spirit of festivity in the woods. This sets the perspective of the play—the celebration of life, the sense of vitality as the central point of reference for man alienated and cut off from life forces by commercialim and materialism. Sukumar is nauseated with this false materialistic life and suffers from depression and melancholia. Doctors, priests and tantriks are hired to cure him of his melancholy, his *bishad*. But he feels they all conspire to make him mad.

The two scenes of seriousness, in which his father, mother, uncles, doctors, priests use all their tricks and persuasive power to attract him to the world and to make him agree to marry are followed by Scene Three that appears funny and humorous. Sukumar with a garland in hand moves from girls to girls, when the fathers of the girls sing the glory of their daughters to the point of grotesque exaggeration. It is a reversal of the traditional practice of Swayamvar, in which a princess has to choose from among the princes who come asking for her hands. This indicates the attempt to reduction to a puppet and his taking the position of a woman suggests his being subjected to a kind of emasculation. At last Sukumar chooses Sundari. This scene is followed by the dance by his wife Sundari trying to lure Sukumar, who remains nonchalant. Her address of love sounds like a parody of the traditional rhetoric of love:

> Sundari: O' the Jewel on my head, O' my dear, O' my lord of my devotion, thou hast for some months been feeling restless just like a fish out of water, *chakor* bird without moon, a lover without her beloved, O' my life... (*Birgati*117)

(Translations of the quotes from *Birgati* are mine).

Sukumar answers in a rather unrhetorical manner undercutting the rhetorical flourish of Sundari and pointing to its hollowness. He says he has no interest in counting coins. If the wealth amassed by his father and uncles is so huge that even in fourteen generations it can not be exhausted, then what is the need for his earning money? He finds himself a misfit. He does not know what to do. He finds himself in a void after rejecting these constricting forces. He does not know what torments him. He experiences an existential angst, an unknowable and unidentifiable, shapeless and formless pain. He wants to live his own life, what Sartre calls being-for-himself not the being-for-others, the life determined and imposed by his father and uncles.

Then some thieves are caught for burglary in the houses in that area and are severely beaten up. Sukumar protests and argues that if, in spite of beatings earlier, they have not given up stealing, then they enjoy beating and also enjoy stealing. Then he develops a strange fancy for stealing, wants to be punished and experience the strange thrill of stealing and of being punished. It is a leap into darkness in search of his authentic self. He then goes on stealing and a prize is declared to catch the thief. But those who catch him, apologise to him when they recognise him as the son of the Sahukar:

> *Annadata,* the sun may rise in the west, the water may catch fire, the sun may change into cool moon-light, mango blossoms may grow on thorny bulbul plants but you can never steal, Sirkar. (129)

He cannot convince them, not even Thakur the village headman, who rather says he is playing a joke or out of sympathy for the real thief wants to take the guilt upon himself. Sahukar asserts that this is a conspiracy against his son and declares that those who are robbed allegedly by his son will be abundantly compensated.

The dialogues between the Sahukar 1, 2 and 3 and Sukumar are an interesting lyrical duet, which is a part of the folk form. Sukumar is stunned that he is not punished, even though he has confessed and there is clear evidence that he has committed the crime of thievery. He ironically feels tortured for not being punished. "What torture you have given me to save me!" (133). He becomes hysterical and sings:

> I am a robber, my name Sukumar,
> I've come out in my hand a sword,
> I am unlucky, oppose me not. (137)

After the announcement by the drummer about Sahukar's promise people, instead of opposing Sukumar, welcome him, when he comes to steal in the night and even invite him into their houses and supplicate him to take something from their houses so that they would be amply rewarded. Even when he threatens to kill any person, they welcome it that the families of the persons killed will be rich many folds for several generations. This is a reflection on our contemporary society driven by commercial greed and perversion of justice.

Sahukars then approach the minister with enormous gifts and request him to do something to tackle the situation likely to be created by Sukumar, who has come out sword in hand to challenge the king. Sukumar arrives at the court and abuses the king saying that the king is a treacherous fellow and he has come to humiliate him. He thinks that that would bring him punishment. When the king becomes furious the minister intervenes and says that he is the son of the richest Sahukar of the town and so being a pampered child he behaves in a strange manner. He rebukes those he really loves and humiliates those he really respects: "*Annadata*, the fact is that he is a fresh young man, who regards insult as respect, abuses as glorification" (143), and he means to say, "Raja you are all great, in your court to you I bow" (143). This is an evidence of how language can be manipulated to the service of the money-power. The king expresses his satisfaction and on the minister's advice appoints him as the marketing officer in the kingdom. Then Sukumar brings out his shoes and beats the head of the king with them and throws away his turban. The minister picks up the turban and shows a dead snake under the turban (which he has secretly put in) and explains that the snake has died from the beating with the shoes. The young man is thus projected as the saviour of the king and the kingdom. The king is pleased with Sukumar, gives him half of his kingdom and marries the princess with him, declares him his heir and also declares him the king. This shows how our present day rulers, the ministers, are stupid and are manipulated by corrupt bureaucrats. The play stops here, does not proceed to tell us what happens after that. It remains an open text suggesting recurrence of such situation in our society.

Birgati is an extended irony. Sukumar's beating up the king is rewarded, not punished. This shows the discriminatory operation of justice in the society, the manipulation of the judicial system in favour of the rich and the powerful even in the society that pledges equality before law. The establishment uses all sorts of strategies of manipulating the situation, manipulating the media to make any rebel, any non-conformist to conform to the established norms. The title *Birgati* is ironical too. Sukumar attains *Birgati* in the sense that he becomes the king considered to be the hero of the kingdom, but in a deeper sense that he attains *Birgati* or martyrdom in his fight against a corrupt materialist society. The second sense raises certain questions – is Sukumar absorbed finally into the established order, or does he continue his rebellion? The characterisation of Sukumar, I can point out, is an instance of neurotic impact of highly materialistic society on young sensitive minds. Another point here is that people are after easy money, disregard all moral scruples as evidenced by the fact that they are prepared to be robbed and even killed by Sukumar, for that would fetch them much more wealth. Common people are themselves complicit in their suffering. Thus Asgar Bajahat's *Birgati* critiques our present day society driven by the complex money-power nexus. The folk tale and folk theatre mode expands the perspective of the play to include the audience, to make them critically aware of their part in this.

Birgati works out an existentialist situation, in which Sukumar searches for his authentic self after denouncing the self and the world designed and determined and sought to be imposed upon him by his father and uncles, and by the society. The play remains an open text indicating that the search continues.

Marathi Drama

Vijay Tendulkar's *Ghashiram Kotwal*

In Maharashtra there are a number of folk forms like *Tamasha, Labani, etc.*, exploited by post-independence Marathi playwrights to represent their sense of contemporary Indian situations. One of them is Vijay Tendulkar, a major voice not only in Maharashtra but all over India.His *Ghashiram Kotwal* marks his break from the naturalist theatre tradition and foray into what can be called the musical theatre. This can be traced to the use of Pirandellian and Brechtian theatre modes – the play-within-play structure and alienation effect in his *Silence, the Court Is in Session*. It presents the rehearsal of a play, which is a playful game that gradually assumes a serious form bringing out the mutual jealousy and hatred of these characters. The anti-illusionist mode thus attempted by Tendulkar is given a new form and dimension through the folk form he uses in *Ghashiram Kotwal*. It makes a contemporary comment through traditional forms. The play is outstanding in the way that Tendulkar brings in various traditions of Marathi theatre and music—the *lavani,* the *dashavatar* and the *gondhal* for his social criticism. The play is apparently an attack on the decadent Brahmin rule in Maharashtra. But this is a reflection on the present-day state of political intrigues, manipulation, ruthlessly self-serving power-game that results in the exploitation and misery of common men. This is also a re-enactment of the myth of Bhasmasur, the demon, who made powerful by the boon of Lord Shiva turns against God himself or Mary Shelley's Monster in her *Frankenstein,* who, a creation of man, becomes a threat to man. In the present-day context demons are initially created by political leaders for the purposes of their power-games but ultimately they go out of control and threaten to destroy their own creators. In the play Ghashiram Kotwal is made powerful by Nana Phadnavis, the Chief Minister of Peshwa, and his disproportionate exercise of power eventually becomes a threat to Nana's position.

Before analysing the play I would like to briefly discuss the Marathi folk forms like the *lavani,* the *dashavatar* and the *gondhal* used in the play. The *lavani* is a metrical composition, which is used for the best part of singing and is characterised by a form of questions—and—answers or dialogue. The *gondhal* is a type of religious discourse presented in a form of recitation or devotional singing associated chiefly with the worship of Shiva and Ganesh and later with Shakti puja. One is secular and romantic and the other ritualistic and religious. Both share the characteristics of dialogue forms to the accompaniment of musical instruments –

tunetune, dholaka, dopli, cymbals, manjiras. The dialogue can be between Shiva and Shakti or between the followers of different cults. Other types of *lavani* are based on purely mundane themes, could be dialogues between two historical characters or the hero and the heroine of a romantic tale. *Dashavatar* is a devotional song accompanied by dance and music depicting the ten incarnations of God. Though they can be called folk forms there is the infusion of the classical in them.

Almost all the characters in these forms sing and dance as they act, as they walk in and out. The characters representing the deities also dance on the stage. *Ghashiram Kotwal* begins with the invocation of Ganapati, Laxmi and Saraswati, in which Ganapati, Laxmi and Saraswati dance. It is in the style of the *gondhal* and the *dashavatar*. The Sutradhar in the play is a folk version of the Sutradhar of Sanskrit drama. In Sanskrit plays Sutradhar introduces the theme, sometimes, the characters in the prologue and delivers the epilogue, but in folk plays Sutradhar interrupts the movement of the drama, comments on the situation for the understanding of the audience and for bringing the audience closer to the stage at the cognitive levels and sometimes plays minor roles like that of messenger. It is through the lyrical form of question and answer with the characters likened to those of the *lavani* and the *gondhal* that the identities and antecedents of the characters are presented. This dialogue between the Sutradhar and the characters at times becomes funny and ironic ridiculing the greed and lechery of brahmins. Brahmins declare they are going to temple but in fact they go to courtesan Galabi's house to listen to the *lavani*, the love song and dance. The contrast between the high religious tone of the opening ritual of the invocation of Ganapati, Laxmi and Saraswati and the hypocritical lewd manners of brahmins points not only to the hollowness of the ritual but also to man's moral decline. The chanting of "Radhakrishna Hari/Govinda Murari/Rama Shiva Hari/ Mukunda Murari" (9) by brahmins on their way to the courtesan's house adds to the irony. The two parallel visuals of the brahmins dancing in Gulabi's house, moving to the back stage and the brahmin ladies and their Marathi lovers dancing in front are indicative of the overall moral decline.

The Sutradhar in his song comments on the present time "The thief is a simple thief/The police are official thieves" (16). In Tanvir's *Charandas Chor* corrupt officials are portrayed like this. In the Ganapati festival when there is going on *Kirttana,* and the Sutradhar as a Haridasa – a special kind of religious story-teller-singer—is singing an *abhanga,* "Nana leers at the women" (18). Nana's lustful chase of the girl, the daughter of Ghashiram after Ganapati worship is over and his taking her away, when Ganapati procession is going on, shows the moral depravity behind the façade of empty ritualism.

In a production note the Theatre Academy comments on the structure relevant to the theme:

> The basic structure of the play is a human wall, which is basically a singing and dancing chorus, impersonally commenting on the episodic developments. But it also breaks into smaller tableau, grouping and regrouping endlessly. The human wall ceases to exist, when its back is turned to the audience. The Sutradhar or Narrator interposes in the proceedings to keep the audience abreast of things, the actors switching parts with perfect timing. A touch of opera with verse, music and prose fusing into one another is a strange, compelling alchemy. The ballet, blending with the traditional folk dances, sets the mood and tempo of the decadent and bawdy era. (Qtd. Samik Bandyopadhyay, "Introduction" VII)

The human-wall formation is taken from *Dashavatar*. It suggests a sense of community life that is fast disappearing and the ideal of collectivity that human society needs now. The blending of various elements creates a kind of ensemble that moves the audience to an awareness of the totality, against which the splintered lives of today are to be judged.

Ghashiram, a brahmin from Kanauj, comes to Poona in search of livelihood but is jeered and insulted by the local brahmins. He manages to become the Kotwal of Poona by weaning the favour of Nana. He then avenges his humiliation and poverty by harassing brahmins and extorting money from them, while Nana in exchange has his daughter for satisfaction of his lust. Ghashiram orders the city dwellers to have permits for everything they do and keep. He, all the time, searches for pretexts, to harass people; even husband and wife are asked to prove their credentials to live together. Like the dictators of autocratic states he makes logic out of illogic. Ghashiram grows disproportionate to his power. He dreams of giving his daughter in marriage to a handsome eligible youth, but it is found at the end that his daughter made pregnant by Nana has died while being aborted. Nana scoffs at his protest mouthing philosophical discourse:

> It is a misapprehension to think that she was here. It was illusion. The body will burn. It is misapprehension to think that she is no longer here. Death is without meaning, Ghashya. Life too is without meaning. (44-45)

This is a parody of high religious philosophical statement and this sense of parody is intensified, I may point out, by the fact that it is spoken by tyrannical lecherous Nana. That makes Ghashiram turn more ruthless and murderous torturing and killing people. When brahmins rise against him and start revolting Nana finds his own position threatened, dismisses Ghashiram and exposes him to the public wrath.

Here the power operates in a Foucouldian sense. Power operates everywhere in a spiralling manner leading to pleasure that leads to power and so on. The source of power remains unidentified and mysterious and, as Samik Bandyopadhyay has interpreted, it operates through masks that become the target of protest and anger, and the masks are changed to pacify, placate rebellion. Tendulkar has shown religiosity and sexuality combining in the strategies of power. Religious rituals are used as a façade for the operation of power. Samik Bandyopadhyay states: "Now he shows sexuality and the strategy of deputation working hand in hand" ('Introduction'-VI). Nana deputes his power to Ghashiram in exchange of his daughter, and when he is of no longer use he throws him away. "Here power is everywhere not because it embraces everything but because it comes from everywhere... It is the name that one attributes to a complex strategic situation in a particular society" (Foucoult *The History of Sexuality* 1976:93).

In *Ghashiram Kowtal* the text, the music, choreography and direction combine to generate a complex and exciting theatre experience. Its uniqueness lies in the combination of the elements of various folk forms, not of a single folk form, to forge a powerful dramatic strategy in evoking the playwright's reading of the present-day socio-religious cultural situation of violence, sexuality and intrigue, power-drive. The play is thus a powerful commentary, on our present day self-seeking power politics, the ruthless exploitation of human sentiments and religious feeling for the agrandisement of power that leads to the suffering of the common man.

3

Post-Independence Bengali and Oriya Drama: Experiment in Folk Forms

Bengali Drama

Bengali and Oriya share many cultural features and folk forms; for instance *pala, yatra* are common to them. Hence they can be discussed together. Bengali theatre has a rich tradition of innovation and experimentation. Rabindranath Tagore in his plays has tried to introduce new modes and techniques. As we find the musical theatre of the present time can be traced to him. Even his plays like *Rakta Karabi* have used folk tale atmosphere, folk modes like *boul* songs in dramatising social and metaphysical issues. Bengali folk forms like *pola, yatra, lok geetika* have been sources of inspiration and material for Bengali plays. The legendary actor Sambhu Mitra, dramatists such as Utpal Dutt, Badal Sircar, Mahasweta Devi, Manoj Mitra, Bibhas Chakravarthy, Saonli Mitra Sisir Das have tried to adopt folk forms in fragments or in entirety in their plays.

Sambhu Mitra's *Chand Banikar Pala*

Sambhu Mitra's *Chand Banikar Pala* (The Pala of Chand Banik) draws our attention to the treatment of a pala, which ivests a folk legend with contemporary significance. Sambhu Mitra is a pioneer of the New Theatre movement in Bengali. He opened a new horizon of Bengali theatre through his production and direction of Bijan Bhattacharya's *Nabanna* in 1944. After he cut off his relationship with Gona Natya Sangh in 1948 he started

Bahurupi theatre organisation and produced a number of trendsetting plays. His production of Rabindranath's *Rakta Karabi* in 1954 is a path-breaking work in Bengali theatre. Apart from many Bengali plays he staged Bengali adaptations of Ibsen's *Doll's House* (Putul Khela), Sophocles's *Oedipus Rex* (Raja Aydipais), Brecht's *Three Penny Opera* (Tin Paisar Pala) which were great success on the stage. His original play *Chand Banikar Pala* is a very popular writing but has not yet been staged. Its cassettes, in which Sambhu Mitra has lent his voice, have become instant hits in Bengal. His daughter Saloni Mitra, a noted actress and writer comments:

> *Chand Banikar Pala* is an extraordinary creation as a drama comparable to epic in its extension and depth. This is acknowledged by all from common man to eighty percent of intelligentsia ("Amar Pratibedan", *Chand Banikar Pala*).
>
> (The Translations of the quotes from *Chand Banikar Pala* are mine.)

The play is a dramatic interpretation of a popular folk tale that celebrates the power of the chastity of Behula in saving the life of her husband Lakshindhar, and that is meant to propagate Manasa Puja (Snake Goddess worship). But this play focuses not on Behula but on Chand, the merchant, and the father of Lakshindhar. It seeks to project Chand's commitment to truth and honesty in a society ridden with corruption and malpractice. The play is interspersed with songs particularly sailors' songs, Manasa prayer and chorus songs that belong in folk tradition.

At the heart of the tale itself there is a conflict, the conflict between the cult of Shiva and the cult of Manasa. While the former belongs to relatively urbanised higher class, the latter is popular among the rural folk, particularly among women whom we can club together as a marginalised group. In the play Chand worships Shiva but his wife worships Manasa and the rural folk worships Manasa. At the end Behula, who gets back her husband's life, spreads the message of Manasa. Chand accepts in the end the worship of Manasa and asserts that it is the wish of Lord Shiva. In the end there is reconciliation between the two cults.

When Chand prepares his voyage the sailors sing of their exciting longing for love and romance, adventure and exploits expressed in colloquial folk style. Ballav, the school teacher, supposed to be the guardian of morality in the society, very ironically dissuades him from this task:

> Look, there is no respect for knowledge, no dignity of education, no gentle manners, no gentle talk. There is no other pleasure than the pleasure of meat eating. Forget, Chandradhar, forget good works. By any means try to save yourself. No gain in running after idealism. (*Chand Banikar Pala*, 23-24)

This exemplifies a fallen decadent society that Chand confronts.

The prayer for the goddess Manasa that Chand's wife Sanka sings depicts her as a Nagini, the dweller of the Nether Land, with her army spread far and wide. Beyond logic, knowledge and light she embodies the primordial forces of life. She is the Goddess of the marginalised community that tries to move to the centre. Six sons of Chand have died from snake-bite. Still she sings:

> Snake-form, snake-shape clad in snake-wear! Beyond knowledge, wrapped in darkness adorned with poison! Embodiment of miraculous energy, O salutation to Mother Manasa! (60)

The voyage of Chand faces shipwreck and all except Chand die. Chand old and haggard, returns home disappointed. His son Lakshindhar has in the meantime become a young man. Ballav and Beni try to persuade Chand to support them in the election so that Beni can become Mahamangalika (mayor) of the city and in return he would be made rich. But Chand remains non-committed and, as a result, incurs the wrath of Beni. He tells Lakshindar, "At least, I am not dishonest, that is my identity" (69).

Two choruses in Act II (part I) informs us Lakshindhar's preparation for the voyage and Lakshindhar's marriage to Behula despite Sanka's warning that he will die from snake bite, if he marries. After marriage they live in a strongly built iron room, specially made to protect them from snakes. On the nupital night Beni's people make a hole in the iron wall and put a snake in. The snake bites Lakshindhar, when in the background Chand sings the hymn of Shiva, and Sanka that of Manasa. Carrying the corpse of her husband Behula moves from place to place praying to gods. In the end she goes to the heaven and gets back his life. There she is asked to worship Manasa and to spread Manasa puja. She then advises people to hold Manasa puja. Sanka too pleads for this. Chand agrees to it at last describing this Manasa puja as a game of Lord Shiva, thus seeing this cult not as antagonist but as complementary to the cult of Shiva. This projects the woman power that asserts against patriarchy but accepts man's power as a part of the universal order.

The assertion of the truth and honesty in the land of lies and deception, and the prioritisation of the rural folk and women in the scheme of the social, and the revelation of the power and strength of woman are the focus of *Chand Banikar Pala*. It celebrates the primordial forces of life, and seems to urge people to acknowledge this and be in contact with this for a vital and satisfying life. It is a *pala*-play, telling a story through narration, song, dialogue and dance. So it presents a community feeling, and suggests solidarity among the people of a community when society is getting fragmented.

Badal Sircar's *Beyond the Land of Hattamala* and *Scandal in Fairyland*

Badal Sircar is a major Bengali dramatist known for his bold experimentation. His *Ebam Indrajit* is an example of absurd theatre depicting the purposeless life of the youths of our time. He has advocated the concept of the Third Theatre, a synthesis of the best elements of the Western and the indigenous theatres. With *Bhoma* and other plays he experiments with street theatre and the environmental theatre. From among the Western modes he was mostly attracted by the Poor-Theatre of Polish director Grotowski developed as polish laboratory theatre. Poor Theatre is called poor because of minimum setting, almost bare stage, minimum dialogue and the emphasis on non-verbal elements – movements, gestures and postures that can build up a stage–image of certain situation, idea or emotion. This is a mode of the physicalisation of emotion that Sircar tries to integrate into his theatre.

Sircar in his two plays, *Beyond the Land of Hattamala* and *Scandal in Fairyland*, uses fairytale aspects of folk culture. *Beyond the Land of Hattamala* (1977) (translated from Bengali into English by Suchanda Sircar) is based on *Hattmalar Deshey*, a novel by Premendra Mitra and Leela Majumdar serialised in the children's magazine *Sandesh* edited by Nalini Das and Satyajit Ray. *Scandal in Fairyland* (*Roop Kathar Kelankar*) written in 1974 for the park, the natural environment, where he usually stages his street theatre under the banner of *Satabdi*, is a fairly close adaptation of the fiction for children written by Premananda Mitra. Though they have adult themes, children should become aware of these. In the process of his dramatisation Sircar has made certain changes to suit his ideological framework and has recast the story in such a dramatic manner that they become typical Sircar plays.

Beyond the Land of Hattamala is a story of two thieves, who fleeing from their pursuers jump into a river and surface in a land where people have never known what money is and where they live by the principle of "from each according to his capacity, and to each according to his needs". It is an exploration of another utopia, an attempt at a redefinition of communism.

When the two thieves, Becha and Kena, jump into the river the four persons pursuing them stand around and become trees. Again these four characters reappear as citizens of the other land where Becha and Kena emerge. This indicates that the new land is an alternative to this sordid world of Hattamala. This is called transformation technique used by American directors like Joseph Chaikin in his Open Theatre mode. Actors become trees, objects and the same actor plays different characters. This is an extension of the Poor Theatre mode. Actor FIVE plays a tree and then an old woman offering coconuts to Kena and Becha and then goes back and becomes a tree. This suggests the natural bond that exists between man and nature. Nobody in this land demands money from them for what they eat, drink or take. When Kena and Becha unused to this practice think they are deceiving people there, nobody bothers about that. They steal but are not caught. With a poker they make a hole in the house but they are not caught and arrested. People rather appreciate their skill in making such a fine hole. Money, payment, they say, are the words they have heard from their grandma's stories about Hattamala. In the library, apart from books, jewellery is kept. People borrow jewellery from it and return them. The library is closed after 10 o'clock at night not for security reasons but for preventing crazy scholars from staying on in the library or sneaking in if the library is open. The Doctor in Hattamala explains that people do their work and get their meals. The chorus at the end sums up this ideology:

> Whatever we need in the world,
> Whatever we can make it all if we work together
> We will share what we have together,
> Come, let's share everything together.
>
> (Beyond . . . 1992 : 132)

The transformation mode used in the play shows the Utopian world constructed as the ideal state that the people dream about their present Hattamala. It is a myth of possibility that dramatist explores. The play presents an alternative myth, an ideal world order that everyman aspires for.

Premendra Mitra's modern fairy tale (*Roop Kathar Kelankar*) is that of a prince and an ogre virtually created by the press and destroyed by the press. The play is "a brilliant critique of the media in their machination for sensation and money" ("Introduction" VII-VIII). Samik Bandyopadhya notes with regard to the performance: "Sircar, for his own performances in the park, made his actors/actresses appear in every day clothes, with a tag on the back identifying the king, the minister, the messenger, etc."(VII). This prevents any possible identification of the spectators with the characters on the stage, creates an alienation effect and provides them a critical perspective to judge the situation.

The play begins with the paper boy announcing the sensational news headline in *Daily Fairy Green* newspaper's extra pullout about Prince Thunderbolt having fought and killed seven ogres, who were eating citizens for their daily meals and having been rewarded halves of the kingdoms. The paper-boy acts as a chorus in reporting the central situation, and he is followed by the chorus of citizens, who discuss and comment on it. This time an ogre attacks fairyland and is about to gobble up the whole kingdom, when the service of Thunderbolt is commissioned on the promise that if he kills the ogre he would get half of the kingdom and the princess in marriage. The sensational tale of the exploit of Thunderbolt and his marriage to the princess boost the sale of the newspaper sky high. The king is a stupid one controlled by the cunning minister, who has vested interest in such news. The same newspaper in its editorial points out that though ogres have been reportedly killed, their corpses are not found anywhere. That leads to public protests and demonstrations and Thunderbolt is called to the court. The ogre is called as a witness. He is "elderly, well dressed, like a gentleman" (40-47). He says he is a simple illiterate ogre, harasses people in Fairyland a little, "crooked men have brought me to this pass, sir"(47). One of the crooked men is a clerk, who pays money to brainy writers to write such false stuff in the paper. He is Midas Speculatorotti, a media-man who creates chaos through false and exaggerated reporting to boost the sale of the newspaper and make money at the cost of the common people. The bogey of Ogre and Thunderbolt are media creation and their fall and disappearance is also media creation.

These two plays illustrate Badal Sircar's theory of third theatre. Eastern fairy tale mode, folk form is blended with Brecht's alienation effect, Grotowsky's poor theatre, American Open Theatre's Transformation mode for commenting on the present day sociopolitical situation characterised by corruption, bribery and manipulation. The sensational journalism to boost the sale of newspapers that create an atmosphere of fear and suspicion in the society leading to conflict and violence is also a part of the corrupt system that the playwright castigates.

Utpal Dutt's *Hunting the Sun* (*Surya Shikar*)

Utpal Dutt's Hunting the Sun (Surya Shikar) is a yatra play. While the yatra is considered purely folk and rural in the context of Orissa, today in Bengal it has gained the status of a highly professional semi-urban theatre, which has made serious inroads into recent developments in modern theatre. The *yatra* must have drawn upon both the Sanskrit tradition and regional artistic forms. "The yatra theatre is rural, semi-urban and urban, and cannot therefore be classified as folk or classical theatre in sociological terms. Its peculiar history with its association with religion, socio-cultural movements perhaps accounts for this" (Vatsayan, 143).

Yatra elements of chorus, songs and *Bidushak* are used in the play *Hunting the Sun* to present an imaginary and historical situation, conveying the conflict between the Puranic worldview and the scientific Buddhist worldview. The situation presented is imaginary historical, for the only historical elements in it are character Samudragupta, a warrior-poet and the challenge to Brahminic Hinduism by Buddhism but all others are imaginary. *Yatra* provides Dutt an aesthetic, theatrical and collectivist mould for his exploration of the vital significance of scientific worldview and scientific learning.

Though there is a Marxist approach evident in the play, the play is deeply nationalistic. Like Galileo of Brecht's *Life of Galileo* the Buddhist scientist is a rebel, who pleads that the earth is round and moves round the sun. By challenging the Puranic worldview Kalhan challenges the entire Brahminic edifice that supports the theory of the divine origin of kingship which has been the basis of feudalism. Though Samudragupta understands the logic of the Buddhist argument and appreciates this, he does not accept it publicly for it goes against the very power structure—the brahmin-kshatriya nexus that his authority draws upon. He rather persecutes Kalhan and his followers just for continuation of the traditional power structure which has been the source of his authority and kingship.

The notion of the purity of the high caste, and even of the divine origin and identity claimed by high caste people, is challenged in the play. Hayagreeva, the mighty general, who conquers kingdoms after kingdoms for Samudragupta claims that he is not a woman-born, he was born from the stem of a tree attributing miracle to his birth and in that sense divinity to his birth. This he uses to establish his supremacy over all others and repudiate the popular notion about his low-caste origin. Indrani interprets that as a baby he was found lying under a tree, so his mother's identity is not known or he may be a son of a Sudra thus negating his high claim of superiority. Hayagreeva falls in love with her but cannot align with her because she is the disciple of Kalhan propagating scientific theory which goes against the power structure he has aligned with. The sexual angle is added to the story as the queen gets attracted to Hayagreeva. For failing to attract Hayagreeva, who has started loving Indrani, she pursues her vengeance. The aura of mystery about Hayagreeva because of his unknown parentage makes him fascinating for women. Indrani is tortured and forced to say that Kalhan raped her, and for refusing to say so she is to be trampled upon by an elephant at the instance of the queen and the punishment ironically is to be executed by Hayagreeva. In the end Indrani along with Hayagreeva dies crushed under the elephant's foot. Kalhan's ashram is destroyed, books are destroyed, but before that Indrani has sent Vivek, the son of a slave to carry away the books she has kept in a village to ensure the survival of the new ideas.

Kalhan is tried but the trial is a stage-managed one. Samudragupta, the wily dictator reads out a letter calling it the letter of confession of Kalhan that the earth is flat, not round, the *Puranas* are true, science is false, God is true, the *Vedas* are true and finally he is a sinner and liar. Kalhan, who has perhaps been drugged then, cannot protest. The king, the establishment, declares him Maharishi Kalhan, an incarnation of God. This is the replication of Buddha being made one of the ten incarnations in Hindu pantheon as an attempt by the dominant culture to absorb little cultures. I may point out that this is how the state uses what Allhussure calls "repressive state apparatus" military, police, etc., and "ideological state apparatus" – school, religion, etc., to dominate the other.

Samudragupta is an ambiguous character—a ruthless dictator and a soft-hearted poet. He is a lonely alienated being, who knows he is surrounded by self-seekers and his wife is unfaithful. So as an escape from this he pursues the pleasures of power. He becomes more poetically eloquent, when he faces a crisis and plans strategies to protect his power. He is caught in what Foucault calls "the spiral of power and pleasure" power leading to pleasure that leads to power. He knows Kalhan is right, and his wife is wrong, yet for power he seems to have ignored all these. To maintain and perpetuate his male supremacy which is required for his feudal authority he turns his blind eye to his wife's illict affair. The power-that-be thrives on the existing social and ideological structure, defined as Brahminic supremacy, caste-hierarchy, the theory of the king-as-incarnation-of God and the superiority of man over woman. Another part of this power structure is provided by the prevailing slave trade that reduces men to the state of the cattle, and gives slave-owners a sense of supremacy and authority. In the slave market they are examined and scrutinised like cattle. Even women-slaves are stripped to examine their beauty and strength. Under the feudal patriarchal structure there is no fundamental distinction between women and slaves. Urmila the queen gets suffocated in the cloistered protected atmosphere of the palace following mechanically royal manners and mannerisms:

> *Dardura:* You see the queen is also a variety of slaves. Jewelled variety.
>
> *Urmila:* I am a prisoner in the palace. And Indrani has taken Hayagreeva away from me. (*Modern Indian Drama*, 604)

Urmila revolts and searches for a life of vitality, that she feels rootless Hayagreeva can give. Indrani's act is a challenge not only to the Puranic orthodoxy but also to feudalism and patriarchy. The play begins with the announcement for the sale of slaves and ends with slave rebellion which indicates resistances building up against socio-political and economic bondages.

Apart from songs and chorus another important folk element in the play is that of *Bidushak*, the jester. He is given licence to comment negatively, even derogatorily, on the king and the queen and the royal parsonages in their presence. He is from a lower class/caste and provides the common man's viewpoint. He is used as a dramatic device, I may say, to subvert the high elitist stances, and introduce common sense approach to the problems. He has also a function of providing comic relief to the audience through his witty humorous comments.

Hunting the Sun pleads for rational scientific spirit, awareness among the oppressed, and opposes obscurantist superstitious beliefs and the autocracy of rulers. Kalhan's ideas survive and spread. Thus he really hunts the sun or search for the sun which stands for truth. Hunting the sun also means an attempt to kill the truth that the orthodox people are accused of. Hunting the sun is also literally related to the traditional theory that makes the sun serve the earth by moving around it. So it is an ambiguous image gathering in itself the opposed meanings and significances, overt meanings being subverted by the underlying significances. It sums up the situation of Kalhan and Indrani, who like Galileo use cunningness to defend and spread the truth like Galileo.

Bibhas Chakraborty's *Madhab Malanchhi Kahanya*

One bright example of the full use of the folk materials is Bibhas Chakraborty's *Madhab Malanchhi Kahaniya* written in 1986. Its uniqueness lies in the reconstruction of a *lok-gitika,* a fairy tale in verse popular in Mymensingh in East Bengal (now Bangladesh), the use of Mymensingh dialect and the *pala* form. This tale of romance between Madhab and Malanchhi in a magical atmosphere is invested with contemporary significance in articulating the woman's struggle for a space in a male-dominated society.

Madhab is the youngest prince loved most by his father and after his mother's death taken care of by his eldest sister-in-law *(bhabi),* Chandraban. After his father's death the astrologer predicts that Madhab will be the king. That sets all other brothers against him and they conspire to kill him. Chandraban comes to know about this and gives him a magic chain that would make him invisible and asks him to leave the kingdom soon. Chandraban as a woman of immense magical power seems to be a character from a fairyland. With this magical power which symbolises powerful intuition, imagination and energy she is a woman of substance, who can go against males in a strategic manner. Madhab then reaches the kingdom of Balaraja, takes rest under a tree, and is found by the *ujir* of Balaraja, taken home and adopted by him. The king takes a liking for the boy and arranges his tuition in the palace by the tutor, who comes to teach princess Malanchhi.

Madhab grows up into a handsome young man. Malanchhi, the king's daughter, falls in love with him at the first sight. One day from the window upstair she throws her quill-feather twice at Madhab standing below, who throws it back twice to her disinterestedly not even bothering to look at her. The third time he turns towards her, throws the quill back in anger and irritation he is soon captivated by her beauty and charm. Then starts the love between the two. Here I can point out that here it is the woman who takes the initiative in love and it is different from the traditional representation of woman merely as an object of erotic attraction.

The love between the two grows but the king, who is unaware of this, arranges his daughter's marriage with the son of Paital Raja. Malanchhi, on coming to know about this, suggests to Madhab to bring a *Manpawan Naa* (the boat of the wind of the mind) that can move with the speed of wind and reach any place that the sailors wish it to reach. In that boat they can flee the kingdom and escape her father's plan to give her in marriage to somebody else. She asks him to bring it to the *gudgudi* tree on the river bank. Madhab soon goes back to Chandraban and tells her everything. His sister-in-law is extremely delighted to see him after such a long time. She soon sends for Kheira, the court messenger, and orders him to go and meet Mona Putar, the carpenter, and ask him to manufacture the *Manpawan* boat within one hour, otherwise he and his family would be executed.

Getting the orders Mona Putar and his sons rush into the jungle to fell trees to get the wood for the boat. Mona Putar sits under a tree brooding over their uncertain future, when his sons go on cutting down trees. On that tree, under which Mona sits lives a *Bengami*, a large, bird with her babies, whose eyes have not yet opened. *Bengami* tells her babies that the carpenter's sons are in search of *Manpawan* wood but they won't be successful, so in the morning they will be executed and if their blood is dropped in the eyes of the young birds their eyes will open. On being questioned by her curious babies she reveals that there are only two *Manpawan* trees - the one on which they live and the other one, on which her husband *Bengama* lives, which is beyond the seven seas. Mona Putar lying under the tree can hear all this. He cuts his finger and drops the blood in the eyes of the baby birds, as a result of which their eyes open and they can see. He then requests *Bengami* for help to save him and his family. Mother bird and children, out of obligation and pity for him, surrender that tree to him and fly away to the tree, on which *Bengama* lives. Here again it is a woman who is given the magic power and insight, and is represented as a kind and considerate being. And also non-humans are given supernatural power and importance which reverses the hierarchy between the human and the non-human. It also shows mutuality and amity between man and nature that is threatened now a days. When Mona Putar and his sons cut down the tree they can see a fire blazing inside it, indicating the miraculous power of the wood. With its wood they manufacture the boat and present it to Chandraban. Madhab in that boat reaches the *Gudgudi* tree and waits for Malanchhi under that tree. When he finds there is delay in her turning up he ties the boat to the tree and goes to the palace in search of her. There he is seen and asked by the king to help him in the arrangement of the princess's wedding. In the meantime another boatman, Hai Chhuina, reaches the river bank in his boat to ferry people for the wedding as per the royal order. He waits for sometime and then goes out to take his food. Returning from the market, by mistake he climbs into the *Manpawan* boat and sleeps. Malanchhi comes in search of Madhab and gets into the *Manpawan Naa*. The magic boat on its own sails away.

In the dark Malanchhi mistaking Hai Chhuina for Madhab speaks amorously to him. When she comes to know the fact she beats him up but has no other way than to sail with him in that boat. They reach Guital kingdom. She sends him out with a piece of her jewellery, and asks him to sell it in the market and buy provisions for cooking their food. But the fellow on the way is lured by gamblers, loses the jewellery in the gambling and is tied up by the gamblers. Malanchhi finding him not coming back puts the guise of a sepoy and goes out to find him imprisoned by gamblers. She offers to play with them, wins in the gambling and gets the boatman released. She sends him back to the boat with the provisions asking him to cook. By the time she herself reaches the bank she finds the boat is not there. Hai chhuina has obviously sailed it away. Then she moves around the market, buys a horse and stays in an inn. Every morning she rides her horse by the king's palace, which is noticed by the *ujir*, a royal official and that is reported to the king. The king impressed by her horse-ride gives her a job in the palace. In the meantime a grave danger comes upon the kingdom. An ogre arrives and eats a man every day and creates havoc in the kingdom. The king declares that one who will kill the ogre will be rewarded with half of his kingdom and the hands of his daughter. Malanchhi plans to kill him. The sepoy hides in the deserted house, near which the ogre comes every day to eat his prey. When that night he comes Malanchhi stabs him with her sword, cuts off his ears, puts them in a bundle and goes to sleep in that room closing the door from inside. In the morning the gardener arrives and sees the corpse of the ogre and tells the king that he himself has killed the ogre. When he is questioned where his ears are, he replies that the ogre had no ears from the beginning. When his wedding with the princess is going to be held, Malanchhi reaches there, produces the severed ears of the ogre. So consequently she is offered the hands of the princess but she says that she has one condition: she will have to get a pond dug up by paying a *kaudi* for each *jhudi* (cane-basket for carrying earth) of earth dug up and after that only she would marry. The work of digging the pond goes on. It goes on for a long time watched and supervised by Malanchhi. It is a case of cross-dressing or transvestism that results in the confusion of identities-man in woman and woman in man. In blurring the distinction between man and woman it rejects the notion that 'manliness' or the attributes of manliness are exclusive properties of man.

Madhab, who has been held back in the palace, returns after sometime to the *Gudgudi* tree and cannot find the *Manpawan Naa* there. He goes in search of the princess, arrives at Guital and comes to know about the digging of the pond. He approaches an old farmer, borrows his *jhudi* and spade and goes for digging. He reaches the site much late and manages to dig and carry the last *jhudi* of earth, when he is noticed and recognised by Malanchhi. She comes out of her male attire and Madhab recognises her too. They are united, tell the king every thing and are given a happy send off.

What I find most important in the treatment of the tale is the central position given to woman. That Malanchhi dressed as a man performs the heroic feats that only man is supposed to do, and be able to do proves that the hierarchisation of man over woman is only a patriarchal construction. The mixed identities indicated by this transvestism suggests overlapping of gender spheres, as we find in Shakespeare's plays like *As You Like It* and *Twelfth Night*. The magic stands for the power of imagination and intuition. The elements of miracle used in the play stand for the tremendous force of the woman's will power, her native wisdom, her imagination and intuition. It is a radical inversion of the traditional tale of male exploits and valour. The play thus, is the product and enforcement of the present-day socio-political agenda of the empowerment of woman. There is also an implied suggestion that nature is the greatest friend of man, and there is need for its preservation and growth for the benefit of man.

The play is in a *pala* form. It begins with a prayer to Alla Niranjan related to the cult of *Satya Pir* or *Pir Baba* followed by both Hindus and Muslims. It projects a community spirit and secular humanism. The characters are presented as human beings not distinguished by any overt religious markers. This tale, thus I can argue, is set to the key of the present-day need for communal harmony. The form of folk ballad Mymensingh *Lok Geetika*, the boul songs, the fairy tale atmosphere, Mymensingh dialects, folk belief in magic all are attempts at the deployment of the indigenous knowledge system to meet the challenges of the sweeping Westernisation of our society. It is a commentary on the present-day situation of women in our society, the struggle of the folk culture for survival against the senseless Westernisation, the loss of our cultural moorings, growing religious and communal hatred, artificial barrier between nations (East Bengal and West Bengal though politically divided are one). It is a total theatre that uses folk tale, folk theatre form, verbal and non-verbal elements, an ensemble of dialogue, action, music, décor and lighting.

Saonli Mitra's Plays

Saonli Mitra's *Nathabati Anathabati* (The Woman Who Has Husband, Has Also No Husband, 1983) and *Katha Amruta Saman* (A Tale Like Ambrosia, first staged in 1990) are bold experimentations in *Pala-kathak* style that seeks to blend Bengali *Pala* style with the *Pandavani* of Madhya Pradesh and Chhatisgarh. Saonli Mitra trained by her father and mother, veteran theatre personalities, Sambhu Mitra, and Trupti Mitra in modern theatre is herself an eminent stage actress. *Nathabati Anathabati* interprets the story of Draupadi, in a different manner as that of a woman who, though she is a wife of five husbands, remains in reality a woman without a husband. *Katha Amruta Saman* is about the plight of women presented through the portrayal of several generations of women– Satyabati, Kunti, Gandhari and Draupadi. For her plays she has drawn upon Kashinath Das' Bengali *Mahabharat* to represent the situation of woman in our patriarchal society.

In the *Pala* form used in both the plays the narrator is a woman played by Saonli Mitra herself. The narrator is called *Kathak*, who is assisted by *judi* or proxy, and the verse passages are sung by the musicians who sit on the ramps or in the four corners of the stage. *Kathak* narrates and sings the verse passages, which are repeated by *judis*. The narration is interspersed with actions, songs, and dances. The last line of the verse is repeated by the *judis* for musicality and for emphasis:

> Sisupala Jarasandha ela Jayadratha
> Tar sange darsakhera ela shata shata
> Aha ela shata shata Nathabati. (10) (original)
>
> Sisupala Jarasandha and Jayadratha
> With them were spectators hundreds and hundreds
> Aha, spectators hundreds and hundreds. (Translation)
>
> (Translations of the quotes from Saonli Mitra's *Nathabati Anathabati* and *Katha Amruta Saman* are mine.)

The "darling of all was Drupada daughter" is the refrain used in the play to show enormity of suffering of Draupadi. Kathak acts out several roles. For instance, while enacting the scene of Draupadi's swayamvar she herself shows the action of Sishupala, Jarasandha and Duryodhana coming one after another with their respective stylised gait, gesture and posture, and raising the bow and failing to hit the target. She depicts the entire range of moods or rasas – *vira* (heroic), *shringar* (erotic), *hasya* (humour), *karuna* (pathos) wherever they are necessary through acting and modulation of voices. *Kathak* is a skilled artiste who makes swift change of roles and voices and expressions to suit the changing characters that she is called upon to portray by the need of the narrative. This aspect of versatility demands the manipulation of all the histrionic and musical skills of the *Kathak* and her *judis*. She distinguishes various characters, for instance, male characters from the female through the modulation of voices and manipulation of gestures. In the play she has been identified as Kathak Arjuna, Kathak Draupadi, Kathak Kunti et al. *Judi* also plays certain characters to assist her in enacting the scene between the characters. This swift change of roles, shift of identity, movement from one character to another serves to underline the roles humans are called upon to play in the world and suggest a general human situation,and, in particular, the situation of woman. Here the actor, not the roles, is emphasised as Brecht's alienation effect postulates. The audience becomes aware of the division between the actor and the roles, and hence are alienated from the action so as to be able to critically judge the play.

The condition of Draupadi is presented in three stages. First, the swayamvara she is won by Arjuna at whom she has loved at the first sight but later on is owned by the five Pandavas in honouring the words of mother Kunti unwittingly spoken. She is used as an object to be enjoyed and divided by males, a food to be shared. "Draupadi, the darling daughter of the king, thus becomes the property of the Pandavas" (*Nathabati* 25). Her wishes are not taken into account; her choice is trampled down; her love is ignored; and she is reduced to a commodity in a patriarchal society.

The second episode is that of Draupadi being staked in the game of dice. She is used as a property here too. Draupadi's question is if Yudhishtir has lost himself in the game first, he has lost the ownership over himself and so has no right to bet her. I may suggest here that Draupadi uses the patriarchal argument to challenge patriarchy itself turning their argument against them, bringing out the bitter irony of the masculinist theory. Bikarna, the youngest Kaurava, raises another question: "Draupadi is not the wife of Yudhishtir alone, she is the wife of other four brothers also. Has she been staked with their permission?"(39). Nobody except him protests when she is humiliated in the court. This is a patriarchal system of justice discriminatory to women.

The Pandavas have their own individual wives Karenumati, Nagabala—Subhadra, Devika, Vijaya—as described in Kashinath Mahabharata that Mitra has followed. Draupadi has loved Arjuna, exchanged garlands with him but has to marry five Pandavas. Essentially she remains alone. It is decided that she will spend one year with each brother, and when she is living with one, if by chance any other brother enters the bedroom he is to be punished with banishment in to the forest for twelve years. Instead of living her first year with Arjuna, she has to live the first year of her married life with the eldest Pandava, Yudhishthira. On one occasion, compelled by the circumstances Arjuna is forced to barge into their bedroom and has to be exiled for twelve years. Then she has to spend her days with Bhima, Nakula and Sahadeva. By the time Arjuna returns he does not come alone, he comes with Subhadra. And during his wandering he has loved Chitrangada, Ulupi and Subhadra. Kathak asks the audience what can be the feeling of Draupadi seeing Subhadra with Arjuna? As the elder one she has to make some sacrifice for Subhadra and allow her to spend more time with him. After the burning of Khandab jungle Arjuna again goes for the conquest of the world. Draupadi has to accompany the Pandavas to the forest in their exile. After Krishna's peace mission fails Arjuna has to travel to places for collection of arms to fight against Kauravas. Then for how many days has she lived with Arjuna? Not many days. When Draupadi is humiliated in the court of Dhritarashtra, Arjuna does not protest. His heroism, his generally accepted role of a knight, is questioned in this context:

> On that day of the ugly game of dice Arjuna was speechless.
> Why didn't he stand for the honour of his beloved Panchali?
> Rather he restrained Bhima. (48)

What kind of man is Arjuna, Draupadi has loved? He has not done his duty as a husband.

Draupadi exhorts Yudhishthira to rise, to be angry. When Krishna goes on his peace mission Draupadi protests that they must avenge her humiliation. When war rages Draupadi finds that it is not a *dharma yuddha*. Pandavas also fight an unjust war even on the advice of Sri Krishna. She wonders, "Is it that to fight against injustice they have to do injustice?"(64). They have killed Bhishma, Karna, Jayadratha and even Duryodhana in an unjust war. Draupadi feels this is not the evidence of heroism of Arjuna. Saonli Mitra deconstructs the notion of heroism of Arjuna. At the time of Aswamedha Yagnya Arjuna goes after the Yagnya Horse and is defeated by Babrubahan. He cannot even save Yadava women from robbers. The entire notion of masculinist ideology is deconstructed here.

Draupadi is haunted by an existential anguish. Her life has become empty, meaningless. "Her life has no justification." Hastinapur has become a graveyard rent by the cries of young widows. *Kathak* at times refers to Irawati-didi to make intellectual comment on the situation. "Drapaudi's suffering is the suffering of an age"(67). She is the queen of Hastina, yet so lonely, so unhappy. The constant reference to Irawati Karve, a famous Maharashtrian scholar of our time, who has made a deconstructive reading of various mythological characters of *The Mahabharat* exposing their male–centred worldviews that exclude, ignore and devalue woman and the patriarchal bias of the author of *The Mahabharata* is intended to relate the mythological text to our modern-day situation.

The third stage is that of her *mahaprasthan*, the supreme departure. She has to go on *mahaprasthan* just to accompany her husbands not for any hope or wish of her own:

> Darling of all was Drupada daughter,
> Now she is the loneliest in the three worlds. (67)

While walking up to the heaven she falls down left and forsaken by her husbands. She only hears Bhima speaking: "Dharmaraj, Draupadi is chaste, Draupadi is incomparable. Does she deserve to roll in the dust?"(69). Yudhishtira replies, "Draupadi loved Arjuna most, she has to suffer for that sin"(69). Draupadi then feels pity for the man, but suppresses all her anger: "This man felt himself deprived all the time, she could not understand this"(69). What has been deep within him has come out at last. He has ignored human sentiment in his single-minded pursuit of the piety, to reserve a place for himself in the heaven. It may be more for his inner emptiness.

There, in the last stage of her life, Draupadi remembers her past days, makes a reassessment of her past experiences. Even towards the end of his life Arjuna marries Pramila. "I die loving somebody, who does not look at me," (71) she complains Yudhishthir remains non-attached. Nakula and Sahadeva are too young for mature Draupadi. As she retrospectively views she finds, it is Bhima, who really loves her but has not been able to express it, whose love she has not recognised and reciprocated properly. It is Bhima who stood beside Arjuna at the swayamvar, when Sishupala and others plan to attack them. He protested when Draupadi was insulted by Duryodhan, Duhshasana, Karna and Jarasandha. He vowed to take the revenge. He carried Draupadi on his shoulders, when she couldn't walk in the forest. He killed Kichak to save her honour. He avenged the insult of Draupadi by killing Duryodhana and Duhshasana. Now at the end it is Bhima, who has put her head on his lap. She hears the grave and lovely voice of the Bhima of the past and the Bhima of the present, "Krishnā! Do you feel much pain? Krishnā!"(76).

She realises she belongs to this world, and Bhima also belongs to this world, whereas Arjun is a romantic philanderer and Yudhishthira is unworldly. With difficulty she tries to touch Bhima's face; the tears of her eyes reflect his face:

> In the next life only you 'll be mine Bhima. Resting my head on your lap I go to sleep peacefully. Only you'll be mine Bhima. You, you will be mine. (76)

This is the realisation of Draupadi that she has loved the man, who does not love her, but has not loved the man, who really loves her. Now in the end she loves him. This is the tragic irony of the play. Draupadi is celebrated in our *Puranas* and *shastras* as *Pratah Smaraniya* (worthy of remembrance at dawn). The greatest irony is that though she has five husbands accomplished with the finest virtues of life she has remained unhappy deep inside her. In a patriarchal society that treats woman as a commodity, as a property, Bhima is a rare male, who recognises her dignity and individuality. Bhima, due to his crude, unsophisticated and rustic way of life remains an outsider to the aristocratic feudal life and, can reach out to Draupadi, marginalised as a woman.

Katha Amruta Samana

The same thematic and stylistic features are found in Mitra's *Katha Amruta Saman* (first staged in 1990). The difference is that in this there is more involvement of *judi* singers. while in *Nathabati* only one *judi* singer joins *Kathak* in presenting the story. The text contains a number of quotations from poet Kashiram Das, Irrawati Karve, Buddhadeb Basu, Maharshi Manoranjan Bhattacharya, Kshirod Prasad Bidyabinod to substantiate Mitra's interpretation of main women characters of the *Mahabharata*, whereas in *Nathabati* she has only referred to Irrawati Karve. Debates and discussion at various stages are made a significant component of the play in the tradition of discussion or problem play started by Ibsen. The reference to modern day thinkers is to posit *The Mahabharata* in the modern context and to read modern situation in terms of *The Mahabharata*.

Saonli Mitra calls it a narrative theatre "Barnanatnak theatre"(8). She has stated that she has studied the folk theatre forms of Madhya Pradesh and Maharashtra, and has experimented in the combination of *Kathakata* and *Natyabhinaya, Kathak thakuran.* Elaborate instruction about the stage direction is given. At the back sit the assistants. The play begins with a *judi* singing the glory of *The Mahabharata* comparing it to the nectar. Then a woman appears playing a mandira, a musical instrument and starts the narration.

A succession of suffering women—Satyavati, Kunti, Gandhari and Draupadi—gives a general picture of woman as the victim of patriarchal order. Satyavati, known as "water–maiden", or "fish-maiden", is loved by Sage Parashar, when she is a girl; a son is born to her but she is deserted by them. Again Shantanu is attracted to her. To materialise the marriage between them Shantanu's son Debadratt, as demanded by Satyavatis father, has to take the fierce vow of the abdication of throne and of celibacy. She has remained an object of erotic attraction for Parashar and Shantanu. She becomes a pawn in the patriarchal game of power and desire. Implicit in it is the suggestion that she has to be a mother of sons, not of daughters, as if to have the full identity of woman. Her sons Chitrabirya and Bichitrabirya die one after another. It is through Vyasa that Ambika gives birth to the blind Dhritarashtra and Ambalika to weak Pandu and the maidservant to Mahatma Vidur, because, except for the maid they all tremble in the presence of Vyasa. Satyavati remains a failure as wife and mother. At the end she, with Amba and Ambalika, goes into the forest, where they die unknown to others.

The episodic structure of the play is maintained as the focus shifts to Gandhari. Gandhari comes from Gandhar rajya, a land of hills and rocks. She has heard her husband is the eldest Kuru, strong and virile; she is amazed to see the Hastina palace studded with jewels and the greenery stretching to the horizon. But when she comes to know that her husband is blind she is shocked and swoons. She then blindfolds her eyes, "she can't see the green pasture, blue sky, red flowers-nothing she can see"(26). Her only wish now is to give birth to the eldest son in the Kuru family, the rightful heir to the throne. But that does not eventually happen.

As regards Kunti Suraraj gifted Kunti to Kuntibhoj, when she was merely a girl, "playing with balls"(28). She was given in marriage to Pandu. Bhishma also chose beautiful Madri as her co-wife. The irony is that Kunti loves Pandu, puts garland around his neck but Pandu loves Madri more. As Pandu has been cursed by a sage that he cannot have any sexual relationship with any woman, Kunti is tormented by unfulfilled sexual desire. Pandu requests her and coaxes her to give him a son, wants her to have a *Kshetraja* son with the help of the mantra that she has acquired from Sage Durbasha. This is a custom that allows the queen to court somebody outside the wedlock to conceive a son for the preservation of the throne, if the king is impotent or disabled. This we have found is used by Surendra Verma in his play *From Sunrise to Sunset* to fashion out feminine identity.

Kunti, through the magic wreath of beads gifted to her by Durvasha, invites Dharma and courts him. Yudhishthira is born. Here the playwright through Kathak discusses the real identity of Dharma. In our *Puranas* there is no divine figure identified as Dharma. Is he Vidura then? Her argument is that another name of Vidura is Dharma and Dharma was cursed to be born as a human. Secondly there was a custom then, still observed in certain places in India today, for the provision of marriage between a woman and her husband's younger brother (*devar*), if the husband is dead or disabled. Devar means *dwitiya bara* (second husband). That, Kathak argues, is perhaps one reason for Vidura's weakness, as we have marked in *The Mahabharata* for Yudhishthira. The birth of Yudhishthira increases Pandu's desire for more sons and Pandu goads Kunti to beget more *Kshetraja* sons (born outside the wedlock). The predicament of Kunti is that, Kathak explains, it is not Kunti's wish, it is the wish of Pandu that Kunti carries out. It is not Kunti, it is Pandu, who decides whom she will accept as her husband. So woman is used as a means of patriarchal wish for preservation of dynasty. Again and make to want women to be mothers of sons, not of daughters. This shows the position of woman not very different from our age, in which the sex-determination of foetus is made and the female foetus is aborted. Madri also has her own son using Kunti's mantra. Kunti takes care of five children but Madri enjoys her time with Pandu in the forest. Once Pandu is not able to resist the attraction of Madri and makes love to her. He is on the spot killed by the arrow that falls on him as ordained by the curse. Madri commits sati with Pandu and Kunti has to return home with five children. When she was a girl she gave birth to a baby from Sun God and put it in a basket and sailed it in the river water. (That baby became Kama, as we know) The irony is that Kunti remains a mother throughout but cannot have the love and affections of her husband.

When Gandhari learns that Kunti's son is the first-born, she wants to go for abortion. The question that is put into the debate by Kathak is, who the real heir to the throne is. One argument is that Pandavas are not really sons of Pandu, they are the sons of Dharma, Pawan, Indra and Ashwinikumar, whereas Duryodhana is the son of Dhritarashtra. So the later is the first-born in the Kuru family and has the right to the throne first. The counter-argument is that both Dhritarashtra and Pandu are *Kshetraj* sons (born outside the wedlock). So why should not Pandu's sons have the right to the throne? Another debatable point is that Duryodhana is the eldest son of Dhritarashtra, who is the king as well as the elder son of Kuru. Yudhishthira is the eldest son of Pandu, who died as a king. Then who has the greater right to the throne?

Another topic that is debated is that whether Karna's challenge to Arjuna is justified. It is not justified, Kathak points out, on the ground of the difference in age. Yudhishthir could be 18 at that time, Karna might be 20 or 21 and Arjuna might be 16. So there is no glory in a 20-year-old challenging a 16-year-old.

The second half of the play is about Draupadi. It begins with *Mulagaan* (the beginning song) addressed to the audience while continuing the narration:

> Listen, listen wise men what happened after that.
> Aha, what happened after that.
> Pandavas get married. (63)

Along with the *Mulgaan* sung *Kathak* utters the rhyme scheme or the *boles* at places, for instance while narrating Draupadi's marriage with Arjuna. She protests when she finds she is going to be the wife of five Pandavas. Yudhishthira gives the instances of Jatila, Bakshi, who had seven or ten husbands, who are remembered as pious women and who lived for hundred. Vyasha and Krishna support him. It has already been discussed in *Nathabati Anathabati* that is she loves Arjuna, who does not reciprocate her love. He returns from exile with Subhadra. She is moved by her affection for Subhadra and asks Arjuna to be more with Subhadra than with her. Then follows her being disrobed, the killing of Kichak by Bhima and the preparation for the war. Gandhari requests Duryodhana not to wage war and urges Dhritarashtra to shun him. Kunti approaches Karna telling him that he is her son, her first-born, he should join the Pandvas. Karna says he was born as a Kshatriya but has no Kshatriya identity and he is indebted to Duryodhana for giving him the dignity of a Kshatriya. He can not leave him at this stage. But he promises he will not kill any Pandava, other than Arjuna. The war turns entire Hastina into a graveyard. After the war is over Kunti with Dhritarashtra and Gandhari leaves for *vanaprastha* and they embrace the fire of the woods there and embrace death.

The play portrays of Satyavati, Kunti, Gandhari and Draupadi as women suffering silently and helplessly. They are used in the games of patriarchal power, live the wishes, pleasures and displeasures of the males, and are denied opportunities to realise their own deepest desires, their inmost being as women. Kathak narrates, acts out the roles and sings alone or jointly with the judi singers, discusses moot points, comments on the story drawing its relevance to the present time, addresses the audience breaking the invisible fourth wall. These two plays are dominated by narrative elements that create an alienation effect.

Mahasweta Devi's *Ajir*

Mahasweta Devi has used in many of her works not only the folk point of view but also the folk style of presentation characterised by a mixture of narration, song, role–playing, playing of folk instrument like dhol. Folk myths and beliefs are used to provide a folk perspective. Her works mainly address the issues of exploitation and marginalisation as a long continuing socio-historical process embedded in social and cultural practices. It is the interlocking structures of oppression, the criss-cross of multiple hierarchies of class, caste and gender that they have been concerned with. *Aajir* can be studied as an instance of her interrogation of class, caste, gender distinctions, which, she has shown in the play, have converged upon the system and tradition of bonded labour ('Aajir' is a Bengali term for 'bonded-labourer'). The study is based on Samik Bandyopadhyay's English translation of the Bengali play *Aajir* (Seagull Books, 1986), which, in turn, is Mahasweta Devi's own dramatisation of her fiction of the same title. 'Aajir' a term usually used to describe an economic relationship, is used in this text for the system of domination and subservience operating at multiple levels of class, caste and gender in the society. Though the play is set in the past it is a representation of the present state of exploitation that continues in spite of numerous legal reforms and defences because of the loopholes in them, and because of the lack of proper implementation of the laws and awareness of them by the exploited.

Mahasweta Devi is a strongly committed social activist, who works among, with and for the downtrodden and her literature is a part of her socio-political programme of action. Poverty, hunger, oppression and corruption in the society move her to action and writing:

> I find my people still groaning under hunger, landlessness, indebtedness and bonded labour. An anger luminous, burning and passionate, directed against a system that has failed to liberate my people from these terrible constraints, is the only source of inspiration for all my writing. (Qtd. Bandyopadhyay, "Introduction". *Five Plays: Mahasweta Devi* IX)

Her literature is political and contestatory in challenging the dominant culture that has, over the ages, legitimised social inequality and oppression. The marginalised people, unable to resist the socio-cultural codes of the dominant, imposed on them tend to internalise those codes and consider them as their culture in defining themselves as the low-caste, untouchables, primitives, bonded-labourers, whores, witches, even as non-humans. These codes reinforce the caste and gender hierarchies and distinctions, and class as an economic factor gets entangled with them. Though caste cannot be exactly identified with class, in Indian society the caste factor contributes to a great extent to the class-division. Low-caste people are severely handicapped by social restrictions imposed upon them, and these restrictions are considered as sacrosanct and inviolable, and come in their path of upward mobility. The element of gender when added to all these multiplies this situation of suppression. An untouchable poor man is suppressed in terms of class and caste, and an untouchable woman is suppressed, at various levels, by men in her community and by men and women of the upper castes. Myths and legends have often been constructed and deployed over the ages to enforce these hierarchies and distinctions of class, caste and gender. The socio-cultural programme of Devi in this context is to deconstruct these hierarchial oppositions and demythicise certain existing myths, which are expressions of the dominant socio-cultural order by exposing all these as partial and political.

The most important factor with Devi is that her literary production is placed within historically specific contexts and her characters are in interaction with historical processes. She calls herself a chronicler, a chronicler of material life and human consciousness:

> Once I became a professional writer, I felt increasingly that a writer should document his own time and history. ("Introduction". *Five Plays* VII)

She tries to trace the genealogy of untouchability, bonded labour, woman-exploitation, etc., and unravel the complex forces operating behind them. She has stated that with specific reference to her texts:

> The history of the past (*Champa, Dewana, Khoimata*) and the history of the present (*Sharers, Dheebar, Pindadan, Jawl, Wrong Number*) both constitute history. There are some histories that are for all times (*Aajir, Stanyadayini*). It is my conviction that a story writer should be motivated by a sense of history that would help her readers to understand their own times. ("Introduction", *Five Plays,* XIII)

But history is a large amorphous text consisting of various and often disparate accounts mediated through historians/ interpreters. So history is as fictitious as fiction. It is relevant here to refer to the theory of New Histori :ism that has attempted to eradicate the distinction between literature and history. Devi's works are chronicles of her time and of the past linked up to the present and also seek to shape the present history. Therefore in her works history and text collapse into each other and what we find in them, to use the New Historical terms of Louis A. Montrose, is "a reciprocal concern with the historicity of texts and the textuality of history" (*The New Historicism,* 1989 : 20).

Devi's five plays *The Mother of 1084, Aajir, Urvashi and Johnny, Bayen* and *Water* all try to subvert the hegemonic order of class, caste and gender. *The Mother of 1084* written against the background of the ruthless suppression of naxalite movement is an indictment of the elitist patriarchal ideology. *Urvashi and Johnny* is an expression of the pitiful life of a ventriloquist, who denied natural love and affection in an exploitative society desperately turns his emotions on his 'talking' doll. *Bayen* questions the stereotypification and segregation of women as witches, as an inhuman patriarchal construction. *Water* is an ironical representation of the tragedy of a dome, who as a water-diviner has to observe fasting and austere rituals to identify the spot where water can be found but, as an untouchable, is denied water from the wells, he helps set up. *Aajir* exposes the system and tradition of bonded labour and develops it into a symbol to reflect on the exploitative and restrictive society. In all these plays, to quote Stephen Greenblatt, culture, as the "ensemble of beliefs and practices ...functions as a pervasive technology of control, a set of limits within which social behaviour must be contained, a repertoire of models to which individuals must conform" (*Critical Terms for Literary Study*, 1990 : 225). On bonded labour in India N.D. Kamble has stated:

> In practice bonded labour in India is the culmination of debtor-creditor relation into slave-master relation. But the bonded labour is an outcome of socio-economic system prevailing in India. Some people who were deprived of socio-economic and political powers had to depend on those who enjoyed these powers. Criminal poverty of vulnerable sections exposed them to exploitations in the built-in mechanism of socio-economic system. Economic dependence and poverty of the under privileged section of the society forced them to be slaves. (*Bonded Labour in India*, 1982 : p.3)

Certain religious cultural codes are devised and/or used to reinforce this economic relationship and give it the form of an inviolable social relationship. The landlord is considered as God or father, legal bond as sacrosanct, ancestral obligation as sacred. The legal bond is transformed into a religious cultural bond. Here Devi's drama experiments with what Frederick Jameson calls the "omnipresence of culture" in which the economics and culture have collapsed into each other.

Paatan, an *aajir*, is the protagonist of the play, who narrates the tradition of bonded labour continuing from time immemorial to the present time and holding succeeding generations in thraldom. That he narrates his own woe proves that he is becoming conscious of his situation and distinguishes him from his ancestors, who have silently suffered. Narration leads to enactment. Paatan plays one of his earliest ancestors Golak Kura, living in the hills of Ayodhya afflicted by famine, who sold himself and his wife Gairabi Dasi away, for a price of three rupees only, to landlord Ravana Sunari. He bound his progeny to perpetual slavery to Ravana and Ravana's progeny. There is a pun on the word "bond", a legal document signed between the creditor and the debtor, and the kinship bond that binds Paatan to the pledge made by his ancestor.

The reference to Ayodhya and Ravana evokes the myth of the *Ramayana*, which in this context has several implications. First, the people of Ayodhya hills (not Ayodhya proper) are the people from the fringe, who are beyond the reach of welfare state, that Ram Rajya represents at its best. There is the reversal of Ayodhya myth here and Ravana remains invincible as the archetypal figure of exploitation as he, not Rama, as the play suggests, reappears in various incarnations. Second, the act of selling oneself and one's wife, that too, in Ayodhya recalls the image of Raja Harischandra, who sold himself and his wife to pay Rishi Vishwamitra his *dakshina*, a customary complementary to the charity he had given. This too has two significances. In the past a king could accept the life of a bonded labourer on oath, voluntarily renounce his kingdom for the sake of piety, whereas present-day rulers are ruthlessly acquisitive and materialist. The second significance is ironical in relation to the present-day context and the main situation of the play, that suggestively questions the very right of Harishchandra to sell his wife, and, by extension, of Ramchandra to put Sita in fire-ordeal. In the same patriarchal tradition perpetuated by upper caste/class Golak sold his wife and descendants, the descendants who were in the womb of the future. So far as the position of woman is concerned she is a slave to her husband, and a slave woman is exposed to all sorts of exploitation by her master and mistress and, as a woman, to the patriarchal control of her husband and her master, the slave owner. She is, in the process, reduced to a commodity, a non-human, an object.

The man with the dhol in the beginning of the play acts as a choric character, who introduces the background and central theme of the play through narration and dramatisation. The evidence of the use of folk elements is the dhol player who is a folk artiste himself, uses a folk instrument the dhol, takes part in folk rituals and performances. As a member of the down trodden community he shares the suffering of the down trodden section, and, as an artiste, has the insight into the tradition, the present situation and has the power to express them. Usually dhol players were employed to announce the arrival of royal personages. Here in the play ironically the dhol player is made to announce the arrival of a bonded labourer Golak. Indirectly it lends a heroic dimension to the stoical suffering of the marginalised. And also the irony emerges from the discrepancy between the style and context, between the formal declamatory manner of presentation and the theme of dehumanising slavery. This creates a sense of absurdity that can be a mixture of pathos and ridicule. The dhol player announces:

> Look at the man, everybody! Bom in a land of famines, nurtured by famines Golak Kura scared of famines has now doomed his descendants to the lives of aajirs. (4)

There is a compounded sense of ironies in the Aajir situation. Ironically Golak Kura is "nurtured" by famines; he is forced into slavery by famine, and the tribe of bonded labourer increases due to famines. Added to it is the fact that people are often slaves not owing to themselves but owing to others, their forefathers. They don't know what is exactly written in the bond that binds them, what its terms and conditions are how far and how long it is legally sustainable. Generations after generations they find themselves in pre-natal and perpetual bondage. Their situation can be well compared with that of the blacks in America. Paatan is in such a bewilderingly incomprehensible world suffering, not being responsible for his suffering and not being aware of the form and shape of the agent that makes him suffer. He is, thus, in a Kafkaesque world that provides him no specific knowledge and reason for his senseless suffering. This lack of knowledge about the context makes his suffering more painful.

The continuity between the past and the present, the grip of the past over the present is dramatically represented by the fact that Golak and Paatan are played by the same actor, and Ravana, the moneylender of the past, and Maatang, the present day moneylender by one actor. That the same actress plays Gairabi Dasi and Maatang's wife, the mistress suggests that slave-woman and the landlord's wife share the same fate of woman in a feudal patriarchal set-up. Paatan's identification with Golak is indicative of his search for the reason for his suffering that continues to delude him even till the end of the play. This technique of playing different roles, which is a significant component of folk performance adds to the alienation effect already introduced through the device of the protagonist narrator directly addressing the audience. Both the spectators and the marginalised made passive under the tradition are targeted. To use the new historicist parlance the social energy thus released is transformed into aesthetical theatrical energy which is circulated back as social energy to the point of origin that is the subaltern.

Maatang, the present-day tyrant, feudal and patriarchal, represents the decadent feudalism – he is infertile, has no issues and has married a woman much younger than him after his first wife died issueless. His infertility is related to the famine that has turned the land barren. He has given the father of his new wife, a sharecropper in his land, a share in his cropland, and has given his wife dowry and promises to give her a son. In that sense he has purchased her. He has married her to have a son from her by some means or other to inherit and protect his property accumulated through usury, land grabbing, filching from government relief. This is how he tries to reduce woman to the body by making her a decorative piece and eventually turning her into a reproductive machine. Women's desire for joyous and free love, suppressed control over their bodies and sexuality is ruthlessly and Paatan's energy and vitality runs counter to Maatang's sterility, his anti-life attitude. Paatan's expression of his desire to marry, have a family and a son of his own inflames Maatang's jealousy, makes him more aware of his gnawing sense of impotence that he desperately tries to hide by flaunting his authority over the former by beating him up. Beating is to reduce him to the body, a beast "a horse" (42) and snuff away his spirit that he fears. Denied freedom and sexual satisfaction with Maatang, his wife, on the other hand, longs for Paatan: "But for me it was a wedding with an old fogey" (46). The Mistress, as a woman, finds herself belonging to a subordinate class in relation to her husband and coming from a poor family she feels closer to Paatan in terms of class-category. She can find in him a potential ally: "Your master has made an *aajir* of you, and of me too" (46). She tries to have some magic potion to control Paatan. She is aware that the existing social gap between the two can be a hindrance to their union. She knows that Bhumihari Dasi, the maid has an eye for him and he is also attracted to a gypsy woman. The knotting of desires for freedom and love, for control and possession cuts across class/caste structures and generates tensions and crosscurrents in the play.

Another instance of feudal and patriarchal subjugation is the case of Punnashashi. The position of town-whore or *Nagarbadhu* she occupies is created and legitimated by the upper class authority. It is an institutionalisation of sexual exploitation of woman. This is a practice, both urban and rural, supported by the folk belief. In this case the distinction between the urban and the rural breaks down. Driven to this profession by poverty she represents the deviant sexuality for catering to the sexual desires of the people of various categories. In order to escape the erotic demands of his young wife Maatang regularly visits her, for it pampers his masculine ego and she does not make any demand for a child of him, as his wife does. But he flares up, when his wife mentions this, branding her as a fallen woman. This notion of chastity is a patriarchal construction to keep women under control; under this system female transgression is punished but male transgression is not; it is rather considered as a male privilege, a sign of virility which is ironical in relation to Maatang. Punnashashi is reduced to an object of sex; she sells her body as commodity. She wants to preserve her body as a human body but let it not to be reduced to the body of the beast, all carnality, and no luminous passion. That's what Maatang does with it in his night-time orgy. It is from the body that she has to perform a very strange ritual. To dispel famine the town-whore is to go naked, pitcher on her head, alone from door to door in the new-moon-night praying for water, and leave the pitcher beside the king's lake and return home, not noticed by anybody. This is a ritual based on folk belief in magic and the power of sexuality. This is a fertility rite that echoes the myth of the sage Rishyashringa lured by whores into the drought-affected kingdom to bring rain. This ritual has turned more bizarre in reducing woman's body to a medium of *tantra.* Punnashashi protests against the torture inflicted on her:

> I have to fast the day through and then roam through the night till the evening star crosses the other end of sky. I can't bear it any longer. (50)

She articulates her feeling of revulsion against the social system, that degrades woman's body:

> Isn't a whore's body a human body at all? You bastards, you had to tear me up, and then I have to fast without a drop of water (50).
>
> Why do you draw the dust from my courtyard for your puja. The famine and the drought come again and again. And the whore has to strip naked and call for the water to bring the rain down on you. (51)

The radical ambivalence of woman is that she is a victim as well as a life-giver, as the Maghai dome, the water-diviner in *Water* is. Punnashashi is another *aajir* made to use her body to entertain people and bring rain to the earth. Because women have been regarded merely as commodities to be exchanged by men, as Luce Irigaray suggests, a woman is divided into "two irreconcilable bodies: her 'natural' body and her socially valued, exchangeable body, which is a particularly mimetic expression of masculine values" (*This Sex* ... 1998 : 180). It is her 'natural' body that Punnashashi wants to defend.

The free natural body is represented in the play by gipsy women. Gypsy women, who sell "magic potion", herbal medicines, show acrobatics, brew liquor, lead nomadic life stand for freedom and vitality in the plays. 'Magic potion', herbal medicines are the elements of folk wisdom. Their free and open air life attracts Paatan from the prisoner's life he leads. While custom and tradition bind the sexuality of Punnashashi, the sexuality of the gypsy women is not. Their possession of the magic potion indicates their possession of the secrets of erotic power that can subjugate men, their ability to activate the erotic power, which is natural and spontaneous, to a mystical level through their participation in the vital forces of life and through intense imagination. The magic potion stands for folk wisdom that can be tapped to revitalise the life atrophied by elitist practices. It is supposed to work miracle like the paste of magic roots given to Rani in Girish Karnad's *Nagamandala* or the consecrate snakegourd representing the phallic God in Chandrasekhar Kambar's *Jokumaraswami.* Maatang orders to drive gypsy women away because they are a challenge to his claim for his masculine authority, and also because of the economic reason that their liquor business threatens his own liquor business. Maatang, a slave-owner, land-grabber, relief-thief, liquor-dealer is identified with materialistic greed and the commodification of all aspects of life that Paatan, Punnashashi, gypsy women and, Mistress oppose. They try to provide an alternative myth, which the Mother of Cremation Ground symbolises, as referred to by Paatan in the play. She is a folk goddess of the marginalised, who stands for the celebration of the spiritually charged body—the body-mystique realised at the meeting of the body and mortality.

The nocturnal ritual performed by Punnashashi that dehumanises woman is disturbed and subverted by Paatan, the gypsy woman and Mistress, as Paatan elopes away with the gypsy woman and is chased by the mob set after him by no other person than Mistress herself. The chorus of the mob reminds him of his perpetual slavery:

> The world's not for you
> The gypsy woman is not for you
> As long as the *ajir's* bond's there
> You're just a maimed beast
> And Maatang is your God
> The gypsy woman's not for you
> The world's not for you
> Life's not for you. (52)

This is a "no-exit" situation of the bonded labour bound by the chains of the past and the blank wall of the future. Mistress promises him his freedom, to give him his bond back and in exchange wants his love. He cannot think that Mistress, so socially and economically superior a lady, can ever love such a poor lowly man like him. Not responding to her overture when he runs away with the gypsy woman she gets him captured and beaten up. At last she steals the bond and they run away in the night. When she hands over the *gamcha* that wrapped up the bond he finds there is no bond, it has been reduced to dust. Suspecting her to have deceived him to make him her slave he, in despair and bewilderment, strangles her to death. The ultimate irony is that no bond has existed but he has slaved away his days without knowing that he is really free Mistress, without knowing that she really has loved him: He kills this, too, suggests that a bond signed many years back has lost its legal validity and practical value:

> Like everyone else in the world I was a free man (Stating a fact) and I alone didn't know. (Looks at the dead woman lying at his feet) this luscious woman was for me, I didn't know (Looks around) (58).

The ending reflects the terribly disorienting effects of slavery. Though Mistress dies at the end she has revolted against the oppressive authority for her authentic self. When Paatan realises his mistake he calmly surrenders to the legal authority.

The play does not end with a doom; it ends with an awareness of the falsity and delusion, on which a slave's life is based. Not only his life but also the lives of his ancestors have been a mockery, he realises. He is confronted with what Althusser calls "absent cause" or Lacan terms "Real" to characterise history, which is inaccessible to us except in textual forms. He is confounded by history, I may say, the history of the bonded labour and the downtrodden reaching him in fragments through multiple layers of textualisation, (re)textualisation – myths, narratives, cultural practices. Paatan at last finds his own subjectivity which is always in flux, defined from time to time by changing structures of power relations by facing up to his situation emerging as a thinking acting being. He recovers his body owned, used and degraded by the master and, by implication, the bodies of his ancestors. He feels the dignity and luminosity of the body, when he realises that his body is desired not only by the gypsy woman but also by the mistress. In India certain practices exploitative in nature continue by the force of conventions, though there are laws against them. The exploitative machinery is sustained by illiteracy and ignorance of the exploited. So the play has no closure, its interrogation of class, caste and gender is a part of the ongoing process of the interrogation of power structures. It denies any distinction between the aesthetical and the political. It is a kind of political intervention, I would like to state, in favour of the marginalised castes, classes and women, an adversial stance against the constricting socio-economic cultural forces, and there is a suggestion to reshape and reform the existing social order.

SISIR DAS'S *BAGH*

Sisir Das is an eminent critic and a pioneer of Indian literature studies in our country. He has also written several poems and plays in Bengali. *Sinduk, Akbar and Birbal* and *Bagh* are his important plays. His play *Bagh,* I find, has used certain elements of folk culture like Tiger Dance – *Bagher Natankii*—popular in the countryside, particularly the tribal areas of West Bengal and Orissa. He has also drawn on the tiger tales found in our folk tales for thematic and technical aspects of this play.

The play is written against the background of the communal riot in Ahmedabad. There is a suggested reference to a tiger, which has escaped from the circus party and prowls about in the town. This is linked up with the *Bagher Natankii* and Tiger tales, which belong to the folk mode. The playwright builds up a fantasy situation but with a strong sense of actuality about it. Two women meet in a deserted house in riot-torn Ahmedabad – one in burkha and another in sari. They are identified in the play as Burkha and Sari. Burkha seeks shelter from the rioter-goondas, and Sari, who has come from the village to the town to see the circus, seeks shelter from the tiger that has escaped from the circus party. Whether the tiger is fictitious or real has not been ascertained in the play. Burkha in the beginning suspects that Sari belongs to the rival group. Sari tells, a rumour has spread that the tiger has reportedly escaped. But there is an announcement by the Diana Company that their tiger has not fled; but the tiger of the Apple Company has fled. Their tiger eats rice and milk, but the Apple tiger eats meat. The voice threatens that if people leave taking it for Diana's tiger they would then set their tiger free. Sari says, that she suddenly saw Apple Company's tiger before her and ran and ran and while running she remembered the tiger-dance in her village. In a tiger-dance a man putting on the masque of a tiger and dressed like a tiger, dances to the beating of the *dhol*. The tiger suggests violence as well as a game. The tiger coming out of a circus party and creating terror indicates that it could have been let free out of carelessness or deliberate design. This implies that communal violence is man-made.

The folk form of the tiger dance with the accompanying songs appears in the play off and on. It depicts the tiger as a ferocious animal as well as an animal tamed by men. Sari recalls two tiger dancers of her village, Binda Fodkiya and Sadhu Jasin. One puts on the mask and dress of a tiger and dances to the rhythmic beat of the dhol (drum) played by another. In the beginning two persons announce the arrival of the tiger and then the dance starts. After Sari tells her tale of running away from the tiger there occurs the tiger-dance and song (pp. 18-19). They sing that the tiger has left the jungle and is in Ayodhya, in the police station implicitly alluding to the Babri-Masjid dispute. There is also reference to 'Sabarmati Babaji' Gandhiji, who laid down his life for communal harmony. Burkha talks about the riot triggered by the throwing of beef into the temple, attack and arson by goondas, and police firing. This is appropriately followed by the second tiger-dance accompanied by the song depicting darkness and gunpowder (23-24). The tiger-dance that punctuates the play is choric in nature in narrating and commenting on the situation. Burkha says, she ran away from the violent mob, entered a house and a woman gave her the burkha. This implies that she is a Hindu helped by a Muslim woman. This further suggests that there are still certain sane elements in the world that has turned insane.

Later on Burkha claims that her village is Pirpur, and many days ago a tiger came to that village. The tiger dancer, who acts as the chorus, sings of the attack of the tiger and a foreign hunter being called to kill it. This suggests how internal conflict once provided an opportunity to the foreign power like the English to occupy and colonise India. Burkha says that she was attacked by a tiger and a man called Mohan saved her but he died fighting against the tiger. Earlier Sari was talking of a tiger, now Burkha talks of the tiger. Hence Burkha and Sari represent the common suffering humanity. Sari hears the voice of somebody, which she identifies with Yusuf. The voice of Yusuf blends with the voice of Mohan implying that Sari was also the victim of communal riot and was saved by Yusuf, who died fighting against the criminals. So here the identities are changed, the roles are interchanged. It indicates women from both the communities are the victims of the tiger of communalism. The tiger dance that follows (31-33) presents the voice of Bagh-bhut (the ghost of the tiger) that describes itself as the ghost of Raktabirya, a mythical demon, who comes alive every time his blood falls to the ground and whose every drop of blood creates demons. This refers to the continual recurrence of communal riots, the seeds of communalism that never die.

In the last part of the play, Burkha, who has earlier mentioned Mohan as her saviour, now along with Sari asks Yusuf, whose voice is only heard, to save them. They appeal to Uusuf-Mohans to come out and fight communalism. The play ends with another tiger-dance-and-song that appeals to fight the tiger of communalism and work for communal peace and harmony:

> It is not yet night the tiger prowls in the town
> I wake up, you wake up, wake up all and one. (36)
>
> (Translations of the quotes from *Bagh* are mine.)

The image of the tiger is built into a multi-dimensional one. The tiger stands for violence and valour. The energy within can be used for destructive and also for constructive purposes. This is suggested by the tiger-dance-song that states that the skin of the tiger can be used for making shoes and Shivaji used its paws as a weapon to kill Afzal Khan, the general of Aurangzeb.

Sisir Das's *Bagh* strikes us with a greater sense of immediacy and contemporaneity than any other plays. The three folk elements – the tiger-dance, the tiger-song and the tiger-tale—are blended to forge one mode and technique. The literal tiger, the fictitious tiger and the metaphorical tiger merge to give a complex sense of the tiger. The characters through their changing dialogues indicate the interchangeability, and mutuality of their experiences. Burkha and Sari are one, Mohan and Yusuf are one. They present the suffering of the common man and continuing fight against the virus of communalism.

Oriya Drama

The cultural landscape of Orissa is distinguished by its various folk forms like *pala, suanga* (musical theatre), *yatra, geeti-natya, das-kathia, desianata, danda-nach, Prahlad-natak, Chhau* etc. Oriya dramatists like Kabichandra Kali Charan Patnaik, a pioneer of modern Oriya drama, Gopal Chhotray, Ram Chandra Mishra, Aswini Kumar Ghosh, Bhanja Kishore Patnaik have shown in their works the evidence of their awareness of the Oriya folk culture. But the conscious and deliberate use of these folk forms as dramatic devices in modern drama comes to Oriya drama after 1970. The playwrights such as Manoranjan Das, Ramesh Prasad Panigrahi, Karttik Chandra Rath, Niladri Bhushan Harichandan, Bijay Kumar Satpathy and Rati Ranjan Mishra are noted for their experimentation in folk forms.

Manoranjan Das's *Nandika Keshari*:

Manoranjan Das is a pioneer of Nava Natya Andolan or Avantgardeism in Oriya drama. He started with social realistic plays like *Jauban* (The Youth), *Janmabhumi* (Land of Birth), *Kabisamrat Upendra Bhanj,* and *Buxi Jagabandhu. Agami* (The Future), *Bana Hansi* (The Wild Swan), *Aranya Fasal* (The Wild Harvest), *Amrutasya Putra* (Children of Immortality), *Katha Ghoda* (The Wooden Horse), *Urmi* (Ripples), *Shabdalipi* (A Game of Words), *Klanta Prajapati* (The Tired Butterfly) are the plays, in which he has made experimentation in expressionism, symbolism and absudism. In *Bitarkita Aparahna* (Encounters in the Afternoon) and *Nandika Keshari* he returned to social realistic themes. Yet *Arany Fasal* (The Wild Harvest) remains his masterpiece and a landmark in modern Oriya Drama.

Manoranjan Das has made full-fledged use of folk forms both content-wise and form-wise in *Nandika Keshari.* This can be traced to his earlier play *Amrutasya Putra,* in which Sanatan, the protagonist, puts on a mask and dances like a character from the *suanga,* or a puppet in the puppet dance to express how man is turned into a puppet by the deterministic routine life. The characters in *Klanta Prajapati* sing like the characters from Oriya Geeti Natya. *Nandika Keshari* is a modern dramatic interpretation of an Oriya legend presented mainly through the folk form of *Desia-nata* (a folk theatre form of Koraput district Orissa) interspersed with many Oriya folk songs, and *pahalis* (folk epigrams) and folk riddles.

This folk theatre form is called *Desia-nata* because it is composed in *desia* language and enacted by *desia* people (*Desia* means anything relating to the village). It evolved as a favourite dance form of the tribals, gradually moved to the royal court and the city, acquired the patronage of kings and aristocrats and consequently imbibed certain properties of the Sankritised urban culture. Its language is simple, comprehensible and meaningful. Chorus is the chief element of this theatre It is full of songs and dances. Sutradhar of traditional plays here is split into two: Sutradhara and Sandhi. Sandhi means truce, so it stands for the link between the stage and the audience, between actors and actions, between characters and episodes. The artistes are to undergo rigorous training for six or seven months in the village *akhadaghar* (the club house for training in wrestling, dancing etc. in the village). The Nata Guru (The Theatre Master) and a group of singers act as a chorus, assist the actor in singing, when the actor performs his acts through acting and dancing. Apart from Sutradhara and Sandhi the characters also sing on the stage. *Gini* (a pair of small sized cymbals), *Karatal* (clapper), and *Khola* (a kind of drum) are used in the play. The play can be staged in any spot that the Nata Guru considers right.

The legend of Nandika Keshari that constitutes the subject matter of the play *Nandika Keshari* is built around Nandika Keshari Patha, a river-island in the river Mahanadi, on the outskirt of Cuttack city, the old capital of Orissa. History says that Cholaganga Dev, who established Ganga dynasty, defeated Subarna Keshari, the last king of the Keshari dynasty of Orissa. Legend says Subarna Keshari was a devotee of Goddess Chandi, the patron deity of Cuttack, and received from the Goddess a victory-gem, which made him invincible. It is said that his minister Basudev betrayed him, and his daughter Nandika stole away the gem and gave it to Cholaganga, and expressed her love for him. But Cholaganga rejected her for her act of treachery and as a result she committed suicide. Subarna Keshari then surrendered and went on Vanaprastha. History and legend are mixed up in the play.

This legend has been interpreted by Radhanath Ray, one of the pioneers of modernism in Oriya literature, in his epic *Nandikeshari* as an evidence of Oriya nationalism by highlighting the heroic virtues, honesty and integrity of Cholaganga Dev and presenting him as a son of Goddess Ganga. When Radhanath wrote this in the beginning of nineteenth century Orissa faced a grave political and cultural crisis created by the colonial rule and the hegemony of Bengali culture, which even threatened the very existence of Oriya language. Radhanath responded to the then need for the rise of Oriya nationalism through the reconstruction of the past glory of Orissa. To project the greatness of Cholaganga Dev, it seems, the character of Nandika Keshari has been degraded.

I can bring here in the perspective of New Historicism (New Historicists like Stephen Greenblatt, Louis Mantrose and George Callaghar have) that states that the power structure of a given time determines the nature and form of discourses, defines what is truth, knowledge, and even what is normal and abnormal. In this light I can argue that this legend has been constructed and propagated by the feudal patriarchal society to legitimise its power and perpetuate its power structure. The myth of Cholaganga as the son of Ganga was thus constructed to make people believe that there was a divine sanction behind the war, the conquest and the rule of Orissa by him, since Cholaganga was a man from the Decan, and initially there could be some resentment against a foreigner as the king of Utkal. This constructed myth and legend could be a strategy, what Gramsci calls, to manufacture the allegiance of the people. In a patriarchal society of feudal nature, a defiant woman is portrayed as mad or morbidly erotic and is sacrificed to uphold the power structure. Nandika Keshari is an instance of this. War is also often used as an imperialist strategy even nowadays to deflect the common man's attention from the real problems of hunger. So Manoranjan Das's play is a re-reading of the legend to create spaces for the woman and the common man in the present-day world.

Nandika Keshari is an anti-war play. The play begins in *Desianata* style with the invocation of Lord Ganesh by Sutradhara, Gayaka (the singer) and Sandhi. Ganesh appears and gives them permission to stage the play. Then arrives Princess Nandika Keshari, who is described by *Gayaka* as a tender girl, whose heart is heavy with grief over the wanton destruction of lives and properties in the war between Subarna Keshari and Cholaganga Dev.

Kalia and Panchua are two *paikas* (Oriya soldiers of those days). During peace time *paikas* were engaged in their occupations in villages and during war they were usually drafted as soldiers. The situation of the common man in a feudal society is presented through the plight of Kalia, originally a fisherman and Panchua, originally a farmer now forced to fight in the war. Through folk songs they express their sad longing for their family, their land, their boat, river and the village greenery. Nandika explains to them how war is futile, how it is a machinery of destruction, and it is a feudal luxury. She finds herself as marginalised as these common men: "I am one of you.... We are one.... Kalia, Panchua and Nandika..."(17).* Finding a kindly companion Kalia and Panchua sing folk songs and dance remembering the feasts and festivities in the village they have left behind.

The shift of scene is indicated by the song of the *Gayaka* that informs us about the break of dawn, and the meeting between Nandika and Basudev, the young minister of Subarna Keshari. They were childhood friends. When they were young they dreamt of bringing about a revolutionary change in society. But the autocratic rule of Subarna Keshari and the war have foiled all their dreams and plans. She now sends Basudev to Cholaganga Dev, whom she considers as an ideal ruler, democratic in outlook. Panchua accompanies him. Subarna Keshari comes to know about this and kills Kalia to prevent the spread of this news of the desertion by Basudev and Panchua that might demoralise his soldiers. Nandika protests against the killing of innocent Kalia.

Another important folk feature is that the play is sprinkled with many *pahalis, dhagas* (Oriya folk epigrams) particularly sung by the *Bayasya* (court jester). Bayasya is a folk character full of folk wit and wisdom, his verses are highly colloquial replete with images from countryside. There is a dream scene, in which Cholaganga sees Nandika, whose portrait he has been shown by Bayasya. This is followed by the appearance of Nandika with the *jaitramani*, the victory-gem of Subarna Keshari, so that his oppressive rule ends and Utkal is ruled by an ideal ruler like Cholaganga and peace and prosperity reigns. Chamupati (the General) informs the king that among the soldiers there has spread indifference and inaction, which is more dangerous than

---

*(Translations of the quotes from Oriya texts are mine).

revolt. This is mainly because of the anti-war campaign of Panchua, who came with Basudev. He preaches "Man is man's brother... Non-violence is the supreme religion" (58). Soldiers have decided to give up war.

Nandika invites Cholaganga then to accompany her to Bidanasi Cuttack, the capital of Utkal, and become its king without causing bloodshed. He cannot accept this, wants to win the kingdom by dint of his valour and does not want to be the king with the favour of a woman. His feudal patriarchal ego does not allow him to accept it. And the most important reason is that Nandika's ideology, her talk of democracy and peace may prove subversive of his feudal imperialistic power structure, which sometimes thrives on war-hysteria. Bayasya gives the information then that Panchua has been killed, evidently by Basudev at the instance of Cholaganga. Nandika is utterly shocked. She finds no basic difference between Subarna Keshari and Cholaganga Dev. They all represent the same feudal patriarchy. There is some hidden alliance between them too formidable for women and common men to oppose. It is she, who has been deceived and betrayed. She has not really betrayed, as it is given out by elitist patriarchal discourse; on the contrary she wants to serve a cause, a cause for peace. She commits suicide then sucking her diamond ring.

The priest then gives advice that instead of cremating Nandika there, Nandika's body should be sent in a *sibika* (enclosed palanquin) to Bidanasi with honour and dignity. It will be reported and publicised that since Cholaganga rejected her love she committed suicide. This will give a clean image to Cholaganga and make him acceptable. The priest describes this as the wish of Goddess Ganga. The dominant class even here invokes the divine wish to legitimise their authority and to explain away this tragedy, and even makes use of this to enhance their image. So the entire legend that denigrates Nandika Keshari is a part of the feudal patriarchal design that Das has tried to expose in the play.

The play ends with Nandika waking up and addressing the audience completing the breakdown of the invisible fourth wall between the stage and the audience. It suggests the recurrence of such subversive forces from time to time to challenge the hegemony of the dominant class. All the folk elements together build up the perspective of the marginalised, and open up several alternative approaches to the contemporary situation.

Ramesh Prasad Panigrahi's *Mahanatak*

Ramesh Prasad Panigrahi is another major Oriya dramatist, whose plays are noted for innovation and experimentation in a variety of modes and techniques. In his important plays like *Mahanatak* (The Great Theatre), *Hatiku Homeopathy* (Homeopathy for the Elephant), *Goonda, Anand Nagarku Yatra* (Journey to Anand Nagar) he has tried to blend realistic, expressionistic, symbolic and absurdist modes.

Here in *Mahanatak* he has used the folk form *daskathia* to interweave various elements and to satirise the dictatorship from the point of view of the common man. Daskathia, a folk form popular all over Orissa, has its origin in the undivided Ganjam district of Orissa, to which Panigrahi himself belongs. The name *daskathia* is derived from two wooden clappers that the singers strike against each other to produce certain rhythmic notes to accompany the songs and verse passages sung by the singers. The *gayaka* (singer) narrates, sings and explains the stories mostly from mythology and the *palia* (the assistant) joins in singing, repeats refrains and responds to the narration and explanations sometimes by putting questions to the singer to ensure clarity and comprehensibility of the subject matter. They play roles of certain characters of the mythological tale in verse that they sing and narrate. The palia sometimes makes jokes, passes humorous comments to provide comic relief to the audience.

Mahanatak was written before the declaration of emergency in India. The play was a dramatic response to the rise of dictatorship, vulgar display of sycophancy, the helplessness of citizens, and the social cultural and intellectual stagnation experienced. It is an extended commentary on the arrogance and stupidity of the people in power. The subject of the play is in the nature of a folk tale, modelled on a popular Oriya folk tale 'The Stupid King and the Minister with a Ball of Straw in the Mouth'. The minister puts a ball made of straw in his mouth to prevent his intelligence from leaking out through the mouth. Panigrahi has written another play *Paka Kambala, Pot Chhata* (Spread the Blanket, Fix the Umbrella) based on the Oriya folk tale of this title.

The two singers of *daskathia* act as the Sutradhar as well as *bidushakas* (court jesters), that are important folk elements and they shuttle between these two identities in and outside the drama-proper. They narrate what they call Bajrabahu Puran that is concerned with Bajrabahu, the king of Hastinapur. The entire play turns out to be a parody of the *puran* (the long verse narrative of mythology), Bajrabahu is a parody of Bajrabahu (Lord Indra) and Hastinapur, of the mythical Hastinapur. The play is a reversal of the myth, an inversion of the *Purana*.

King Bajrabahu declares himself "the most handsome man", "the mightiest emperor in the world" (8). Everyday he sees the reflection of his face on the water kept in an earthen pitcher. He is highly narcistic, trapped in his self-love. But with the increase of his arrogance the size of the earthen pot does not increase. This unalterable shape and fragility of the earthen vessel suggests the reality that is limited and constrictive. The king claims himself to be the source of all thoughts: "Why should the citizens need the faculty of thinking, when we're the king of Hastina Pur?" (8) It echoes George Orwell's novel *1985*, which describes "thought control" as a component of the dictatorial system. Educational institutions are closed down and acharyas are made to carry bricks and stones, for these institutions are the breeding grounds for new ideas. He commands to sell knowledge in the foreign land and earn money. The *daskathia* singers then turn into *bidushakas* and try to gain the favour of the king through flattery, to which, they know, the king is susceptible.

As a reversal of the natural order the court sits in the night time, that too, in the royal entertainment hall. Absurd complaints come up and fantastic judgments are delivered. Karnat Raj complains that there is no peaceful co-existence between hands and feet of the citizens and they cut off each other's hands and feet. The king orders that the hands and feet of Karnat Raj should be cut off. These would sprout on their own. Gouda Zamidar complains that in the evening women disappear and fishes turn into girls. The king's solution is that if women are drowned in the river, they will be fishes again. That shows the degradation of woman in society. To the complaint that there is rain without cloud he orders to construct a ceiling under the sky. All these unrealistic occurrences belong to the fairy tale world which indicate utter disorder and confusion in the natural and organic order that reflect social political disorder.

Bajrabahu is impotent, the queen is issueless, all married women in the kingdom are barren, and all youths are weak. It is a wasteland. To cover up his impotence and emptiness he inflates his ego by exercising excessive power over the subjects making them work as bonded labourers in his dream project of constructing a ceiling under the sky. This echoes Ravana's attempt to construct a ladder to the heaven. The arrangement of the most glittering silver jubilee celebrations of his reign is intended to divert the attention of the subjects from the issues of hunger and poverty. He sings:

> I distribute plenty of nights
> Long dreams of thousands of miles. (41)
>
> (Translation of the quotes from the play are mine)

The queen Ketakigandha representing the women community is tormented by the hunger of the body and heart. Her cry mingles with the cries of sexually subjugated women and hungry subjects. Abanti Sadhab is another character, who appears as a dream merchant as a contrast to Bajrabahu. The dreams he sells are to satisfy this hunger but the dreams the king sells is to avoid hunger. Abanti Sadhab secretly meets Ketakigandha. They sing and dance together in a musical duet depicting the postures of the dancers on the walls of Konark and Ajanta, expressive of the union between two romantic human beings thirsty for love.

> Here rise the dormant nerves of Hastinapur
> With dreams many a thirst is quenched. (45)

This awakening of vitality becomes a precursor to rebellion. Ironically the bidushakas, through flattery, hastens the process of the fall of Bajrabahu and serves as a catalystic agent.

There is an interesting and fantastic encounter between Bajrabahu and Dead Man. Dead Man represents the men, who have died from starvation under the misrule of Bajrabahu. This presence of a ghost is indicative of the powerful role of the past in shaping the present revolution and also of the sense of fear and insecurity that haunts Bajrabahu. Brahmadatta leads the rebellion, the king is brought down from the throne. The earthen vessel breaks down suggesting the collapse of the king's large-sized ego. There is a dramatically ironic ending to the play. King Bajrabahu declares his own punishment in a rhetorical manner. He sentences himself to death in a royal style. It is another pathetically ridiculous expression of his haughtiness. The futility of haughtiness is proved but its elimination is not assured. It suggests that there is no complete end to tyranny; there is only a temporary pause and the struggle for change goes on.

The mingling of solemnity and ridiculousness, seriousness and banality, grandiloquent style and trivial sentiments makes it a powerful irony, a satire on contemporary socio-political situation. This play can be compared to Albert Camus's *Caligula* but white Caligula's act expresses man's indomitable spirit, a spiritual, metaphysical aspiration *Mahanatak* remains a socio-political satire.

Kartik Chandra Rath's *Bahniman*

Kartik Chandra Rath is another significant voice in modern Oriya drama. *Jiban Yagnya* (The Yagnya of Life), *Swarga Dwara* (The Gate of the Heaven), *Darpan* (The Mirror), *Samudrara Ranga Yantrana* (The Colour of the Sea is Suffering), *Bahmiman* (The Spark), *Trutiya Pruthivi* (The Third World) are his important plays. His plays represent the common man as a protagonist fighting against exploitation and injustice. To articulate the common man's situation the dramatist has been in search of common man's idiom, and in *Bahniman* he locates it in Oriya Geeti Natya (Musical Play) popularised by Baishnab Pani, Jagannath Pani, Mohan Goswami, Gopal Das and others in the nineteenth century Orissa.

Oriya Geeti Natya has wider folk appeal, enacted by village people, popular in villages. It contains lots of folk elements – folk characters, idioms and expressions—and also classical Sanskrit elements because of the influence of Sanskrit texts. This blending of two cultures was itself exemplified by its major exponent Baishnab Pani, who, though a Brahmin, had lived with a washerwoman, a low caste woman, and was declared an outcaste. There are prologue and epilogue presented by Sutradhar along with singers. The actors deliver dialogues, dance, sing and act in stylised gestures to the accompaniment of music.

This play has followed the structure of Geeti Natya with *Prastabana* (proposition or prologue) and *Nirbahan* (conclusion or epilogue) with four chapters in between. The *prastabana* begins with a Sanskrit hymn invoking the Sun God and with a dramatisation of the conflict between light and darkness in the heart of man. Light and Darkness and Man are represented as characters. It is an allegory that echoes the similar scene of the conflict between Good Angel and Bad Angel for the possession of Dr. Faustus's soul in Marlow's *Dr. Faustus*. Darkness promises him properties, happiness, sexual pleasure, and light promises him truth, virtues, justice, insight. Man accepts both. In the play Man is split into two – the king and the subject, the zamindar and the peasant, the capitalist and the labourer. This charts out the four stages of human civilisation – monarchy, feudalism, capitalism, and post-capitalist technocracy, represented in four subsequent scenes called "chapters" in the play. The king, the zamindar, the capitalist and the technocrat are played by one actor; correspondingly Bidushak, Gumasta (zamindari accountant), the Manager and the Machine Assistant by one actor. The subject, the peasant, the labour leader, the beast of burden in the corresponding scenes is identified by one named Bhadra, played by one actor. So also is the case with the princess, the daughter of the zamindar, the daughter of the capitalist and the daughter of the Technocrat identified as Mitra in these scenes. These analogies and correspondences emphasise the similarity of human situation over the ages and continuing struggle of the common man against oppression and exploitation.

The first chapter begins with the song of Sutradhar comparable to the song of Duta. Duta, the Messenger in the court of Kansa, Ravan et al is a popular figure in Oriya Yatra and Geeti-Natya. He is very down-to-earth and colloquial and sings in folk rhythm. He acts as the royal messenger, reports the off-stage occurrences and comments on the contemporary situation like price rise, social inequality, exploitation that affects the common man. Duta is mainly responsible for relating the past to the present, the mythical to the contemporary. He has the licence like Vidushak to criticise the higher ups even in their presence.

Sutradhar introduces the theme of exploitation and symbolically declares that he will show "the drama of the tiger and the stag" (17). In the Geeti Natya style the king, Bidushak,

Bhadra and Mitra enter with stylised gait and stylised gesture. When poor man Bhadra approaches the king for help, the king in an exaggerated style asks him in return to give him wealth, power and happiness, heavenly elephant, Paradise flowers, the sun and all the comforts of life. Mitra, the princess makes Bhadra conscious of his due rights. Bhadra rises in revolt against the king and is killed at the end.

In the second chapter Sutradhar in the beginning sings of zamindars, who are no less cruel than kings. Here Bhadra is a peasant, who is encouraged by Mitra, the zamindar's daughter to rise in revolt. His revolt ends with his being captured and beaten up, while he goes on protesting. The third chapter begins with a folk song by Sutradhar that describes a capitalist society, in which the capitalist turns exploiter. Street singers called *caranas* usually sing this kind of song and have a role in arousing the consciousness of common people. Bhadra, the labour union leader, rejects all temptations, even the offer of his daughter's hands, and rises in revolt. Mitra, the daughter of the capitalist, joins Bhadra in his agitation. In the fourth chapter Sutradhar's song depicts the age of technology, in which man becomes a slave of the machine and is reduced to a beast of burden. It is futuristic in implication. Here again the common man Bhadra is inspired by Mitra, the daughter of the technocrat, to use his own creativity and become the master of the machine. Bidushak, Gumasta, Manager, Machine Assistant in all the episodes play sycophants to their masters.

The first chapter is mostly presented in the form of a series of songs dramatically rendered suitable to the nature of the characters and situations, because it represents the old medieval society and it acts as an introduction to the play. All other chapters are realistically structured with only one introductory song in the beginning. There are a series of vignettes repeating the same story in different contexts.

In the last scene Nirbahan a spectator comes to the stage and addresses the audience. He wants to assert that they face the same predicament as that shown on the stage. This reinforces the alienation effect built up successively by the Sutradhar and other methods adopted in the play. The absence of any demarcating line between the stage and the audience in a folk performance is suggestively used here to extend the stage to the audience and carry forward the revolutionary ideology.

Niladri Bhushan Harichandan's *Kaluribenta*

Niladri Bhushan Harichandan, an eminent poet and critic in Oriya, has also published several plays that have been broadcast in All India Radio, Cuttack. *Jatayura Chhinna Dena* (The Broken Wings of Jatayu) is a collection of three short plays *Kaluribenta, Jatayura Chhinna Dina* (The Broken Wings of Jatayu) and *Arana Mainshi Rahichhi Anai* (The Unruly Buffalo Is Staring). *Kaluribenta* is an Oriya folk tale in verse, which is used as an underlying structural pattern in the play *kaluribenta* to convey how justice eludes the honest common man, making him run from pillar to post.

This short folk narrative-song depicts the plight of a crow. A crow wanted to eat Kaluribenta (Kaluribenta is a fruit), Kaluribenta advised him that he should go and wash his beak first. The crow then beged for water of a well. The well asked him to bring a pitcher to draw water. When he went to the potter's house for the pitcher, the potter ask him to get the earth from the field for making a pitcher. The field asked him to get the horn of the stag for digging the earth. The stag told him that he should get for him the milk of a black cow, so that he could drink the milk and be strong enough to give him his horn. When he approached the black cow, the cow asked him to bring grass for her. For grass he went to the meadow and the meadow told him he should have a sickle to cut the grass. He went to the blacksmith's house. The blacksmith asked him to wait for a while and then he put the hot iron sickle in the beak of the crow. The poor crow died then and there. Every time the crow approached somebody he would sing of what the previous ones had wanted him to do. In the end he sang before the blacksmith:

> Give me, O' blacksmith, give me a sickle!
> Let me cut the grass,
> Let the cow eat grass and give milk,
> Let the stag drink milk and give me his horn,
> Let me dig the earth with the horn.
> Let the potter make the pitcher,
> Let me draw water from the well,

Let me wash my beak,
And then let me eat Kaluribenta.

Chorus:

Caw, Caw, Caw
Kaluribenta is the fruit of the sky, eat, eat, eat!
Wherever you go, you hear no, no, no.

(1998 : 3–4) Translations are mine)

JATAYURA CHHINNA DENA

The chorus is repeated in all the ten scenes to reiterate the theme of the honest common man's fight and failure at different stages in the present-day corrupt bureaucratic society. This folk song is woven into the body of the play as its structural pattern.

Guru Charan Behera represents the common man in the play, an honest chowkidar working in a dak bungalow in an Avayaranya, the forest in which animal killing is strictly prohibited. One day a high-ranking officer sahib comes and stays in that bungalow, gets an animal killed and arranges a feast with his friends and orders Guru to cook it. Guru refuses to cook that food, protests against animal killing, applies for leave and leaves that place. But his application for leave is rejected. Guru also informs the authority about this unlawful killing of animal. On the contrary he is put under suspension on the ground of insubordination. Then Guru has to run from pillar to post to get justice and also to get his due from the government. Guru approaches the superior officer but is refused any help. The officer says:

> I am bound up in the community of our officers. I have no strength to free myself from this trap. If any officer commits any injustice, other officers will definitely try to cover it up. There is no question of willingness or unwillingness. The community interest is more important.(22)

The dealing assistant concerned says:

> Has anything been done here without any offering? Of course I don't need. But others won't leave. Certain percentage of money for the purpose will have to be paid in advance. All will have a share in it. (24)
>
> (Translations are mine)

He does not pay bribe and cannot get his due.

The play is a satire on bureaucratic red-tapism, under which the common man gets crushed.

There are some similarities between the folk song and the situation of Guru and by extension the situation of the honest common man in the present day corrupt society. But our attention is drawn more to the differences between the two levels of narrative – the folk and the contemporary—and these differences point more glaringly to the unjust, inhuman social order of our time and honest man's sufferings and humitations within this.

BIJAY KUMAR SATPATHY'S *EI JE SURJYA UEN* (*HERE RISES THE SUN*)

Bijay Kumar Satpathy is one of the younger Oriya playwrights after independence. His important plays are *Fasilra Nidrabhanga* (The Awakening of the Fossil), *Kanshara Atma* (The Soul of Kansa), *Kshyudita Sarisrupa* (The Hungry Reptile), *Ei Je Surjya Uen* (Here Rises the Sun) and *Pralaya Pare* (After the Deluge).

Satpathy's play, which is noted for the use of folk elements, is *Ei Je Surya Uen*. It is a dramatic exposition of exploitation that appears in different forms in different ages. The traditional forms that are used in the play are that of Oriya *pala*, a folk form and the song of the *caran* (wandering minstrel) which is a part of Oriya popular culture.

In Oriya *pala* there is a *Gahana* or a *Gayaka* (the main singer) and four or five *palias* (assistants), the chief of whom is called *Sri Palia*. *Sri Palia* takes the lead in the follow-up to the singing by the *Gayaka*; he sometimes makes humorous comments and tells jokes to provide comic relief to the audience. One of the *palias* plays the *mridanga* and is called *Bayaka* (one who plays the drum) and other *palias*, the *jhanja*, (cymbals), *gini*, (small cymbals) and clappers. They usually put on *chudidar* and muslin Punjabi. The *Gayaka* is more glitteringly dressed. He carries a *chamar*, which he waves while singing and dancing, and which he often uses as a sword, —bow or — mace in his enactment. The *Gayaka* supported by *palias* sings, narrates and explains and even dramatises the stories from mythology. He embellishes them with quotations and illustrations from the works of Oriya poets such as Upendra Bhanj, Kavisurya Baladev Rath, Abhimanyu Samant Singhar, Dina

Krushna Das, Banamali Das, Radhanath Ray, Gangadhar Meher, Madhu Sudan Rao and many others.

Ei Je Surjya Uen begins with a prologue (*upodghata*) followed by two scenes called *Prathama Parba* (first section) that deals with exploitation in the feudal age, and *Dwitiya Parba* (second section) that deals with exploitation in the present age. These two scenes enact the same situation only in different forms and contexts. There are similarities even between the names of the characters; for instance Bajraditya, the king of the first section becomes Aditya, the capitalist in the second section; Srikantha, the revolutionary poet of the first becomes Kantha Das, the trade union leader in the second. So the same actor plays both Bijraditya and Aditya. The case is similar with other two parallel sets of characters in the two parallel scenes. The stage is divided into two zones. The change of place and time is indicated by the change of action from one zone to another. The props can be minimal and suggestive.

The prologue of the play consists of two parts relating to the two scenes representing the two ages – medieval feudal age and the modern age. As the first zone is gradually lighted the chorus that is played from the background becomes clearer and louder. The music stops. An extremely poor, sick and weak man is seen tottering up onto the stage. Sitting down with much difficulty he brings something out of the bundle he has carried on his shoulder, when the sound of drum beating and slogan shouting is heard: "Victory to the Maharaja..." The food drops from his hand, when the king's thundering voice is heard:

> Yes, you are the accused. Your poverty is your crime. There are so many criminals like you in my kingdom. Only rich aristocratic people have the right to live here. Your place is in the prison...(*Ei Je Surjya Uen*, 1987 : 1-2)
>
> (Translation of the quotes from this play are mine.)

This strikes us as the cruellest irony. The man then runs from one side to another and then runs in a particular direction. Joining his two hands in the posture of being handcuffed he runs. Tired and exhausted he sits down with hands on the head. It suggestively shows the suffering of the common man in a feudal age. The second part of the prologue indicates the change of context to modern age and the change of roles with slogans like, "Fulfil our demands", "Labourers unite" being heard. The man on the stage gets excited but has lost his speech. He expresses his anger and excitement through gestures and postures. Then there is the sound of the gun, the whistle of the police, running about helter skelter. The man runs from one zone to another and falls down tired at a particular spot. From the background come the voices of the lawyer and the judge indicating that a case is being heard in the court. The man is charged with stealing factory properties, instigating communal riot and indulging in terrorist activities. The man is sentenced to two-year rigorous imprisonment. The man rises slowly, with his hands linked together in the posture of being handcuffed, and he walks slowly. These two pictures in the prologue provide the framework of the play presented mostly through mimes. The expressive potentiality of the non-verbal is exploited in the manner of Artaudian Theatre of cruelty. What is implied and suggested in the prologue is expanded in the two succeeding scenes.

The play-proper begins with a pala form. Only *palias* are on the stage playing *Khola* and cymbals rhythmically. Each player then walks with certain peculiar gesture, which is humorously commented upon by others. This is followed by the invocations of Goddess Sarala, the Goddess of knowledge worshipped in Jhankad, Orissa and of Lord Narayan. Then the *Gayaka* narrates in verse the oppressive rule of Biraditya in traditional *pala* style assisted by *palias*.

Biraditya is a whimsical tyrannical king of Karnapur surrounded by sycophants. The minister, the general, the court jester and councillors keep the news of people's sufferings away from the king apprehending that it would bring discomfort to the king and make him be annoyed with them. A luxury palace is being built, when people are dying from starvation. Poet Srikantha Das in his poetry exhorts the people to rebel. He is imprisoned and tortured. His beautiful wife is imprisoned. The queen opposes this and is killed. This section ends with a rebellion led by Sadhu Charan that leads to the arrest of the king and declaration of democracy. All these actions are compactly packed into a short span of one scene, and the pace of the action is very swift. In one sweep it takes in the entire range of the feudal age.

Has already been the second section is about the modern capitalist age. This is suggested by the second part of the prologue. It begins with a song sung by street singers of *caran* type– one carrying a picture fixed to a pole, the second one a harmonium, the third one a *mridanga* and another person following the singer in singing. This can be categorised as a part of popular folk culture. The *Gayaka* has a bag slung over his shoulders and holds some booklets in the hands. The *pala* players of the last section appear as street singers in this section. This scene is usually seen in the streets of towns and cities. Short narratives in verse on some sensational occurrence in the society are printed and sold in this manner. The style is the style of *Malika* (Poetry of Prophesy about the coming of Kali Yuga written by medieval Oriya poets like Achyutanand) that appeals to people's imagination. In this section the medieval Karnapur becomes Karan Pur. The scene changes to a city.

King Biraditya becomes Aditya Pratap, the industrialist; Bailochan, the court jester is Lochan, the Sarapanch; Surya Sen, the general is replaced by the Manager; Srikantha, the poet is Kantha Das, the trade union leader of the present age. But Sadhu Charan of the past is transformed into Sadhu Charan, a corrupt minister, Mandhata and Jay are the politicians, who represent the courtiers of the first section. Mandhata draws his pension as a freedom fighter on the strength of false certificates. The same actors play similar and parallel characters. The labourers suffer and starve. They are suppressed and tortured. There is labour strike led by Kantha Das. Jagabandhu, another labour leader is used by the company to break the strike and is killed by company men to falsely implicate Kantha in the charge of murdering him. Kantha Das is imprisoned. His beautiful blind wife Malati is forcibly taken away from the labour colony and sent to the Minister Sadhu Charan. After being raped Malati is killed. Kamini, who resembles Kadambini the Queen of the first section, protests against this and is killed. Kantha breaks the Jail, turns into a terrorist. When he tries to attack Aditya, he is shot at from behind by the police and is killed. But his defiant voice of protest rises.

The play ends with the visual of the rising sun and the man carrying a torch and shouting and moving from one end to the other. It ends with a mime which is highly moving and poignant.

It ends with a note of hope, with the march of the indomitable spirit. It is a powerful critique on the present-day exploitation and corruption.

The first section is in the form of a folk tale, an invented story; the second section is that of reality. The play suggests that the machinery of exploitation remains same; there is only change of roles and contexts. The form of the *pala,* whose singers in course of singing and narration act out different roles, is the appropriate framework for the play that uses role playing as a significant dramatic strategy. Satpathy in his other play *Sonita Sanksha* makes an atempt at interpreting another form of folk tale-*Osha Brata katha* (The Tale of Ritual Worship).

There are many other Oriya playwrights who have experimented in the use of folk forms. Rati Mishra's *Satarka Sanghamitra* (Cautious Sanghamitra) is an example of the blending of myth, folk legend and folk custom and belief. Rati Mishra's *Satarka Sanghamitra* is based on the folk custom of *Kumari Kanya* (girl-goddess) mostly observed in Nepal. According to this custom a ritual search for the girl to be anointed as a Goddess is conducted and ends with the discovery of the girl with certain divine signs and the girl is worshipped as a goddess, say goddess Durga for certain period of time. The girl remains a spinster all through her life even after her period of incarnation as the goddess is over. Over the years quite a good number of women, who have played goddess in their lives, live lonely single life without adequate physical and economic support. Many of them are sexually exploited by the feudal class and thrown away as they become old and many take the path of prostitution. In Orissa parallel to this are the practices of *Kalisi* in rural and tribal areas. This is the customs of somebody being chosen as a medium to be possessed by a deity. Rati Mishra, while severely critiquing such a practice, uses it to expose exploitation and corruption in the society and project resistance building up against this. Added to this folk is the fact that people were forced by the tyrannical king of Keonjher to dig a canal without wages. As a result a large number of people died from starvation, exhaustion and ill-health and they, it is believed, turned into fishes constantly wailing their woes in the canal that became a river later on. This river in Keonihar is called *Machhkandana Nai* (River of Wailing Fishes). This Kumari Kanya (living Durga), through the design and machination of the king is sought to be used by him against the rebel leader Parasar, whom he depicts as demon Mahishasur, and ultimately turns against him and destroys him. Ironically the king turns out to be real Mahishasur. The myth of Durga is blended with the folk culture. There is a reference to another Oriya folk myth and legend. It is that of Biswabasu, who is presented in the play as the narrator and as a sort of ideologue of resistance against exploitation. The legend says that Biswabasu, was a tribal king who first kept Lord Jagannath and had been worshipping Him in a cave. Later on King Indradyumna with the help of his Brahmin minister Vidyapati stole him away to Puri and installed Him there. So Jagannath is considered originally as a tribal deity appropriated later on by Brahminic Hinduism. Biswabasu as the narrator who arouses people against exploitation represents the higher consciousness.

4

Post-Independence Assamese and Manipuri Drama Experiment in Folk Forms

From the Northeast of India I have chosen only Assamese and Manipuri plays, because the plays from other regions are difficult to collect either in original or in translation, and their languages are beyond my comprehension. Assamese and Manipuri have rich folk as well as literary traditions and share many cultural features. Particularly the influence of saint poet Shankar Dev goes beyond Assam. The *Ankia-nata* of Assam started and developed by Shankar Dev has also contributed to the development of *rasa,* in Manipur.

Assamese Drama

There are two important traditional folk theatre forms in Assam, *Ankia-nata* and *Oja-palli,* that have attracted the attention of post-independence Assamese dramatists. The three important plays discussed here are Arun Sarma's *Buranji-pat* (Reading from History), Satish Bhattacharya's *Maharaja* and Yugal Das's *Bayanar Khol* (The Drum of the Drum Player in *Ankia-nata*).

Arun Sarma's *Buranji-Pat*

Arun Sarma is one of the pioneers of avant-gardeism or Nava Natya Andolan in Assam. *Nibaran Bhattacharyee* is his first successful play. It is about a veteran actor who is found delivering dialogues to an empty auditorium pouring out his pent-up emotions of frustration. This shows the indifference of people of today to the theatre and the disillusionment of playwrights and theatre artistes. *Ahar* and *Chiyar*, are his other important plays.

In *Buranji-Pat* Arun Sarma has used *Oja-palli* style. *Oja-palli* is a musical narration accompanied by acting and dance. The *Oja* is the Chief singer, who sings and narrates the stories mainly from mythology and is assisted by *Daina-palli*. This is like *pala* in Orissa and West Bengal. In this particular play Bairagi, the *Oja* is a narrator as well as a character who moves around making people conscious.

The play was written against the background of the emergency in India in 1975, when individual rights were curtailed and the press was muzzled. The play is a response to as well as an allegorical representation of this situation. The folk perspective becomes complete, as it is presented in the manner of a folk tale. The action of the play takes place in Kanchanpur, which consists of 42 hamlets and has been under the administration of the ancestors of Kulahari Chowdhury. Kulahari joined the freedom movement and lost the maujadari (Zamidari) of the village to Jalaluddin. Due to partition Jalaluddin faced problems in managing the estate, and his brother Badruddin managed it on his behalf. Later on, on the advice of Jalaluddin, he returned maujadari to Kulahari Chowdhury family. His son Narahari was given the responsibility. But in the midst of the celebration of regaining maujadari Narahari passed away. His widow daughter Priyarani then takes over the charge of mauja. Priyarani with the help of her friend Bhuyan and her son Chandan starts a reign of terror in the mauja. Corruption and misdeeds become rempant. Bairagi, the *puja-palli* singer, goes around from house to house singing folk songs narrating the plight of the people. At last under the leadership of the old man Kulahari Narahari's sons and the people of the village rise in revolt.

In *Burandi-Path* we find that an imaginary folk tale and *oja-palli* are invested with a contemporary significance. *Oja-palli* singers narrate as well as comment on the situation. It is a critique on autocratic tendency of our present day rulers.

Satish Bhattacharya's *Maharaja*

Another important example of the use of *Oja-palli* form is Satish Bhattacharya's *Maharaja*. Paramanand Rajbanshi, a pioneer in the experimentation of the folk form in Assamese drama has in his introduction to the play explains why the title of the play is "Maharaja" instead of being "Maharaj". He argues Bhattacharya has chosen the title following Kamrup dialect. There is also another reason, which is ironical. In the village influential, proud and arrogant people are called raja. The term is a satirical reflection on them. Like Arun Sarma's *Burandi-pat* the play represents the conflict between autocracy and democracy.

The subject matter of the play is an invented folk tale. Pratapaditya is the old king of Surya dynasty. Though he has two sons, the king marries his beautiful maidservant Ganga and promotes her to the position of his queen. The story begins with the arrangement for the coronation of Bikramaditya, the son of Ganga. But subjects get enraged at Bikram's rape of Malati, the daughter of a peasant Jagatbandhu, and march to the palace. The king is compelled to put off the coronation. The king has two ministers, Satya Narayan and Buddhi Narayan. While Buddhi Narayan is generous and is devoted to the cause of the subjects, Satya Narayan is a self-seeking opportunist person. Malati is kept as a maid in the palace. Without the knowledge of the king, at the instance of Ganga Malati's father Jagatbandhu is imprisoned and tortured. Bikram lets loose his reign of terror. The subjects led by Amrit Narayan as their leader rise in revolt.

Satya Narayan, on the advice of Ganga, invites Amrit to the palace and tries to win him over but fails. At this time Buddhi Narayan and Majaraja enter and the king allows Amrit to present the grievances of the people. The king, then, can know the atrocities committed by Ganga Dasi and their prince, and accept the demand of the people to hold election. In the election Amrit is elected the Prime Minister and the subjects are allowed to take part in the administration.

After this another conspiracy is hatched in the palace by Ganga Dasi and Satya Narayan. Attempts are made to paint Amrit Narayan as treacherous to subjects. In the meantime Buddhi Narayan, who after retirement as a minister has become the king's advisor, is assassinated and Amrit is shown to have been involved in it. With his presence of mind Amrit foils this conspiracy. It is through the promptness and intelligence of Malati, though a maidservant in the palace, that Satya Narayan and Ganga Dasi are exposed and convicted. The assassins are sentenced to fourteen years imprisonment and Satya Narayan to a lift-term. By announcing that Bikram will not be made the king, the king gives the subjects the right to rule. The old king remains the nominal king in the state but democracy is established. The play is about the fall of autocracy and rule of democracy. The palace intrigues conpiracies, manipulations and corruptions reflect our present socio-political reality.

This is an imaginary story narrated by *Puja-palli* and other singers. The play is punctuated by songs and acting. Prose dialogues, songs, narrations and comments give it an intricate structure.

YUGAL DAS'S *BAYANAR KHOL*

Yugal Das's *Bayanar Khol* (The Khol of Bayana) uses as well as deals with the *Ankia Nata*. *Ankiya* is a popular form of traditional theatre with lots of folk elements created and popularised by Shankar Dev. A social reformer, poet, musician, dramatist and drama director Shankar Dev has unique contribution to Assamese society. The performance of *ankia-nata* is called *bhaona.* Gayana and Bayana are two important figures in *ankia.* The former sings, the latter plays the musical instrument Khol (a type of drum called mridanga).

The play "The Khol of Bayana" stands for *anika-nata,* and so for the tradition of Assam, which is scorned by the present day youths. Every year on the birthday of Shankar Dev *ankia-nata* of Sri Shankar Dev and his disciple Madhav Dev expressing the Vaishnavic tales of Vishnu are staged in the village. It is Bayana's duty to go around and arouse and invite the people to make preparation for and join the performance. This year the younger generation wants to stage a modern proscenium stage play. That sets off the conflict. Bayana practises playing Khol every day. That day he awakens the people by playing his Khol for preparation for *ankia-nata.* His own daughter, who is supposed to play the heroine in the modern drama proposed to be staged, opposes him. The tension continues for sometime but it ends with a note of reconciliation. The elders feel that it is not possible to resist the change and the youngers realise that the old cannot be totally ignored. So it is decided that both the *bhaona* and the modern play will be staged. Bayana's passionate commitment to his art and the sweeping change brought about by modernism provide the dramatic tension. That the play is presented in *ankia* style is itself the evidence of the need for exploring folk wisdom for facing up to the modern situation.

Manipuri Drama

This section on folk elements in the post-independence Manipuri drama is based more on performance pieces than on written texts as in the cases of other dramatists. It is because the playwrights, I have chosen, are writer-director-producers, who have concentrated more on performance aspects than the written text. The theatre that evolves is called the Physical Theatre closer to the Polish dramatist Grotowski's "poor theatre" that emphasises the physicalisation of emotion, the configuration of movement, physical gestures and postures to convey some patterns expressive of emotions and thoughts. Manipur has a long and rich tradition of martial art. Manipuri drama and dance naturally draw their resources mostly from this non-verbal cultural expression that the martial art tradition provides. Artaud's Theatre of Cruelty also exploits the physical and the American Open Theatre mode entails upon the actors rigorous physical exercises. So Ratan Thiyam and Kanhailal have not exactly turned to the West but have resurrected the culture of the body that has a long tradition in India to express their sense of the world around.

Ratan Thiyam's *Chakravyuha* (1998)

The pre-text and reconstructed text of Ratan Thiyam's *Chakravyuha* prepared by Kavita Nagpal published by Seagull Books is the basis of my study. It is difficult, I admit, to have a full comprehension of the performance without seeing this; still then some sense of Thiyam's unique dramaturgy can be made out from what Nagpal has presented. *Urubhangam* (1981), his own *Chakravyuha* and *Karnabharam* (1989) constitute Ratan Thiyam's the *Mahabharata* triology. They are all produced by the Chorus Repertory Company organised in Imphal. Violence and the question of identity are the continuing concerns of Thiyam. Abhimanyu, who has trusted his technique so fool hardily, is a symbol of the younger generation. The predicament of the not so well equipped younger generation in a world torn by senseless violence is the theme of the play. Thiyam has taken the model of Bharata's *Natyashastra* for his play but has interfused it with Manipuri folk narrative art.

The form that is used is that of *Wari Leeba*, a traditional form of narrative art in Manipuri, particularly of the Hindu *Puranas*, the *Mahabharata* and the Manipuri chronicle. In the *Wari Leeba* the narrator narrates sitting with one or two bolsters as his props and what comes out is a typically Manipuri version of the *Mahabharata*. The clothes, flowers, eating habits and even sub-plots woven into the main text are distinctive to Manipur. He has given also a human angle to the *Mahabharata* through the *Wari Leeba* mode. Vyasa's characters are larger than life, whereas Thiyam's is closer to everyday reality. The *Wari Leeba* paints pictures in words. Sutradhar in the prologue describes first the essence of the Natyashastra, the aesthetics of performance and the entire first fourteen days of the war in the *Wari Leeba* tradition.

The *Wari Leeba* is not the only source. He says, " For the Arjuna-Subhadra scene I go to the most beautiful narrative singing style of Manipuri called *pena* ("Introduction" *Chakravyuha* XXV). There is a special portion in the *pena* called *leirol* where several types of flowers are described. Another important source material for speech in the drama is *Lairif Haiba Thiba*, a narrative form performed by two characters. In it one actor narrates the original text and the other interprets it. The modulation of speech and the use of different pitch patterns create its own drama.

When in the beginning of the play Drona prays to 'Tulsi' and Kaurav as enter, the music that is used is from a festival conducted by priestess called *Maibis* to propitiate the sylvan gods, who are considered as the preservers and creaters. The dance of Maibis is called *Laiching Jogai* (*Laiching* dance). Thiyam has made rigorous study with the best guru of the Nat Sankeertan. He has drawn his resources from religious texts in different ragas and raginis (rhyme scheme) and rhythms and dances of different patterns or *cholons, the Pug Cholons*, the *Thang-Ta* and drumming.

All these Manipuri traditions he has drawn upon but used them in his ways to create his own tradition. He takes the basic elements, rhythms, but alters them in such a manner that though it is familiar its effect is uncommon, an element of surprise is introduced. He says:

> So you see I am trying to relate to tradition not as a dead artifact but as a living throbbing beautiful part of my heritage. I cannot replicate it since I live today and whatever is expressed filters through my modern sensibility shaped by contemporary influences. (Qtd. Nagpal 'Introduction' XLII – XLIII)

Ratan Thiyam's theatre is thus an attempt at an eclectical appropriation of the traditions of both the East and the West for the expression of the Manipuri situation. He has successfully blended the Sanskritic theatrical tradition formulated by Bharat with the Manipuri folk style.

The Theatre of K.H. Kanhailal: *Pebet*

The discussion on Kanhailal's Pebet is based on the performance–piece of the play prepared and edited by eminent Indian theatre critic Rustom Bharucha. I am indebted to Bharucha for his extensive introduction to the two texts *Pebet* and *Memoirs of Africa*. While Thiyam emphasises the director's role but does not altogether rule out the controlling factor of the written text, Kanhailal gives the director the final say. Thiyam has stated:

> The moment I become the director, the playwright in me goes away..A director's thinking is very different from a playwright's thinking... But the director has no right to create whatever he likes, stepping out from the playwright's point of view. (Qtd. Kavita Nagpal, "Introdution". *Chakravyuha,* XII)

Kanhailal's theatre assumes that the written word of the dramatic text does not, indeed cannot determine the overall meaning of a performance, which is constituted through the juxtaposition and blending of different elements and individual inputs. The second difference between the two is that while Thiyam's theatre has quite a good amount of dialogues and songs with greater emphasis on light, sound and stage décor, the idiom of Kanhailal's is predominantly non-verbal and gestural with very few dialogues.

The most important difference between them is that Thiyam's plays address the Hindu culture, mainstream Brahminic Sanskritic tradition. Vyasa and Bharat are assimilated into

Manipuri tradition by him. Kanhailal is concerned with the exploration of the ethnic identity of Manipuri, the existence of a distinct Manipuri identity and culture before its Hinduisation.

The main contributing factor for Manipuri identity and ethnicity is the awareness that politically and economically Manipur has remained a much neglected state, even after so many years of independence. There is large scale poverty and unemployment. Corruption is the major cause of its backwardness. In the words of Manipuri poet L. Somer Singh "corruption in Manipur has become a way of living, a kind of ritual. Without it you would not be able to do anything" (Qtd. Bharucha, "Introduction," The *Theatre of Kanhailal*, 13). There is anger, militancy and even separatism. Kanhailal talks of his Meithei identity. There was indigenous culture of Manipur prior to Vaishnavite movement of the eighteenth century, which was strongly propagated by ruling monarchs like Garib Niwaz (1709-1748) and Bhagyachandra (1763-1798). The traditional *lai* (gods) were destroyed, ancient scripts, the Meithei scripts were burnt and replaced by the Bengali script, the Hindu calendar and system of *gotras* were introduced, Hindu dietary laws were enforced. Still then the ethnic culture is available to us as "traces".

The prevedic Meithei deity Sanamahea continues to be worshipped in every Manipuri household or that ancestor-worshipping festival like the *Lai Haraoba* continue to be celebrated every year. The main point is that the ethos of Meithei culture has been systematically subsumed within the value of an increasingly powerful Hindu hegemony. Historically the people of Ningthonja class were called Meithei. They later on subdued the other six classes of the state around AD 33 to form a community. In the late 60s and early 70s of the twentieth century pre-Hindu Meithei-Meithei religious groups emerged to counter the dominance by Hindu-Meithei Vaishnavaites. There was movement of resuscitating the past by re-affirming the worship of Sanamahea in opposition to the Radha-Krishna culture. There was resistance to the imposition of Bengali script and move for the revival of Meithei script. These involved a conscious rejection of Hindu values and artifacts, even the wearing of tilak and the dancing of the *Ras* as Vaishnavite impositions. The political goal of the movement was the establishment of an "autonomous Meithei state". Also there was movement for the liberation of Manipur from "Indian occupation".

Along with this overtly revolutionary activity there was cultural counterpoint provided by the Pan Manipur Youth League (PANMYL) founded on ethnic identity, Meithei–tribal ethnic oneness. Kanhailal's *Pebet* is closely related to the ideology of PANMYL. But there is diffusion of ethnicity in his later works like *Memoirs of Africa,* because by then the resurgence of Meithei identity has lost its edge. The movements were suppressed and so there was subdued violence. Kanhailal's youngest son was imprisoned for this involvement with this insurgency movement, and he was tortured "Violence however subdued, almost invisible has become the omnipresent banality of Manipur"(Barucha, 20).

Kanhailal's actors have to undergo rigorous training because the non-verbal elements dominate his theatre. Sabitri, his wife is the centre of his theatre. The training of Kanhailal's actors to a large degree is based on the physical culture of Manipur itself. In *Thabal Changba* dance they dance through the night during the Holi celebrations linking their hands to form a large circle, building a communal energy and rhythm with strong, vigorous jumps. The martial art tradition *Thang-ta* too has served as a source of inspiration to many of Kanhailal's exercises characterised by the lightest, most spring-like movements. Kanhailal's plays *Tamnalai* (Haunting Spirit) in 1972, and *Kabui Keioba* (Half Man Half Tiger) in 1973 were the products of the political and revivalist fervour of the late 60s and early 70s. They are the subversive interpretations of Manipuri folk tales to express the struggle for ethnic identity.

Pebet, as a tale, is a part of *phunga wari,* or fireside stories, which are told to Manipuri children by their grandmothers. It is a folk tale deeply entrenched in the psyche of the people. Kanhailal has used this as an excellent dramaturgical strategy to comment on the political and cultural indoctrination of his time. As Barucha has summerised, the folk tale is about Pebet, a bird smaller than a sparrow, which has not been seen in many years. Guarding her brood Mother Pebet averts the predatory attention of a Cat by flattering him. She continues with this technique. Her children grow up and are ready to protect themselves. Once they are grown up she resists the Cat. But the Cat captures the youngest in her brood. Ultimately through a clever strategy the mother manages to trick the Cat into freeing her child. The Pebets are finally united. The Cat disappears somewhat dejected.

In Kanhailal's play the first and last parts of the story are left more or less intact. Indeed the few exchanges of dialogue between the Pebet and the Cat are borrowed verbatim from the oral tradition of the story. He breaks with the tradition of Pebet in the middle part of his production after the youngest child has been captured. Here, he develops a fantasy sequence in which all the Pebet children are captured, indoctrinated, tortured and then set against one another. This is the policy of divide and rule that the hegemonic power employs against the subordinate class.

Pebet is not an animal fable. The Cat himself is something of a sadist, who enjoys playing with his prey before killing it. Kanhailal's Cat is clearly Vaishnavite in his rhetoric and tactics. The most savage irony of his indoctrination occurs when he brainwashes the Pebet children with the famous words from the Sanskrit sloka:

> *Janani Janmabhumischa Swargadapi Gariyasi*
> (Mother and Motherland are superior to the heaven.)

Using these Sanskrit words as weapon the Pebet children turn on their mother and stone her pitilessly. This is a parody of the famous Sanskrit lines.

It is wrong to consider Pebet "anti-Hindu" and dismiss it as "anti-Indian". At no point does the play attack the idea of patriotism or the love for one's motherland. Barucha argues:

> What Kanhailal is questioning are the cultural formations through which concepts of patriotism and loyalty are imposed. In the name of *Janmabhumi* (and not *Ima Leipak,* which is the Manipuri word for motherland), the cat uses his language and strategy to make the Pebet abuse their own mother. (34)

It is the totalitarian nationalism that ruthlessly ignores the regional specificities and that the playwright questions. In a different manner but in the same vein Hayavadana in Girish

Karnad's play *Hayavadana* questions the efficacy of grand nationalist discourses in solving the problems specifically local. He finds that he is not able to be complete in spite of his reading in nationalist discourses. The real fear of mother Pebet is not that the Cat will eat her children, but rather they will be converted to the 'Cat-culture'. Kanhailal recalls one of his early inspirations *Luxun Thongba,* a ceremony in which a young man is formally initiated to the Vaishnavite faith through a conglomerate of rituals, fasting and begging that make the boy and his relatives cry (source: Barucha, 34-35). The boy is seen crying through rituals and Kanhailal questions if the boy is forced to initiate. These rituals, are parodied in the sequence where the children are converted into the Cat-culture. But the process of indoctrination is disrupted when one of the Pebet sons bites the Cat's arse instead of licking it. This is one of the few instances in the play that leads to torture and eventual freedom.

For a start, as mentioned by Barucha, there were seven actors representing the Pebet children, who were differentiated through the colours of their turbans, which in turn were associated with the seven *salai* (class). These have formed the basic social structure of the Meithei people from their earliest history. More significantly there were two drummers positioned on six-foot scaffolds. They observed and participated in the action. One of the drummers was played by Kanhailal himself, who intervened in the action of the play at a critical point as an ancestral figure, the Old Man of the Village. When the mother was stoned by her own children, the Old Man would respond to the cry and carry her on his back placing her on the scaffold. Reacting to the action, the Cat would throw him down from the scaffold and torture him. This was to imply that the Pebet could be destroyed only if the spirit of the village was eliminated. All was not lost, of course, because Mother Pebet would emerge once more as a powerful figure holding on to a flag. The flag was made up of seven pieces of cloth from the turbans of the actor. It served as a symbol of resistance, a reminder to the Pebets that they must continue to fight for their identity.

Later productions did away with all these colours and flags because no such rigid ethnicity was the issue. Kanhailal's flexible dramatic idiom can adapt to the changing situation.

Ratan Thiyam and Kanhailal, we find, use folk elements for different purposes, representing two different cultural currents of the region, the Hinduistic tradition and the ethnic pre-Hinduistic tradition. Though both use the technique of minimalism in their theatre, put emphasis on light, sound and décor, Kanhailal's is more physical, gestural and non-verbal.

5

Post-Independence Kannada and Malayalam Drama: Experiment in Folk Forms

Kannada Drama

Two important playwrights in Kannada after independence who have effectively used various folk forms in their drama are Girish Karnad and Chandrasekhar Kambar. Karnad has used *Yakshagana* style and interpreted a Sanskrit folk tale in *Hayavadana,* and a Kannada folk tale in *Nagamandala.* Kambar has been consistently experimenting in folk forms, interpreting different Kannada folk tales using *Yakshagana* and *Bayalata* forms.

Girish Karnad's *Hayavadana*

Girish Karnad in his landmark play *Hayavadana* (1971) has made an effective use of the elements of folk culture to subvert the hegemonic discourses and dominant ideologies structured around the traditional assumption that head is superior to body. Based on Thomas Mann's *The Transposed Heads* (1940), a fictional interpretation of a Sanskrit folk tale about the switching of heads taken from Samadeva's *Kathasaritasagar* (written around AD 1070) and presented in *Yakshagana* style the play deals with the polities of head and body to explore a wide range of cultural politics, which is fundamentally concerned with the legitimisation of social relations of inequality and the struggle to transform them. *Hayavadana* works through various hierarchical oppositions such as man/woman, upper class caste/lower class caste, the elite/the folk, even human/non-human subsumed under the head/body opposition and repudiates the notion that the first components are identified with head, soul, spirit, reason and are superior and the second components with instinct, materiality, sexuality and are inferior. Also relating to and underlying them are another set of oppositions such as the west/the non-west, the Aryan/the pre-Aryan, the nation-state/community states, Sanskritic scholaticism/Bhasa literary traditions.

As a playwright, actor and director working for theatre, film and TV, Karnad has a wide range of experience and training in various modes and media and has the cross cultural background to be deeply aware of these dualities at various levels:

> My generation was the first to come of age after India became independent of British rule. It therefore has to face the situation in which the tensions implicit until this had come out in the open and demanded to be resolved without apologia or self-justification, tension between the cultural pasts of the country, and its colonial past, between the western mode of thought and our own tradition and finally between the various visions of future that opened up once the common course of political freedom was achieved. (Jaydipsinh Dodiya Ed. *The Plays of Girish Karnad: Critical Perspectives*, 21)

By "the cultural pasts of the country" it is meant the vital pluralistic culture of India represented by various cultural forms and by "the colonial past", the Western impact and hegemony that is questioned by the natives. The past that the modern writers seek is to be significantly related to the modernity, to a local sense of progress and human freedom, and hence to "the various visions of future." Without that the affirmation of the local through the celebration of the past often results in "localism" or "Third Worldism" as Arif Darlik has pointed out (1996). Karnad, being conscious of that, uses history, myths and folk forms of India to address the contentious issues of class, caste, and gender, and of the social differences amplified by the present socio-economic conditions.

Folk forms, we know, are the expressions of the universal of the local. Folk tales, songs and theatres are mostly authorless or have fictitious or multiple, unidentifiable authors allowing enough space for listeners/readers to open and close the text's signifying process without being constrained by the signified. Because of the multiplicity of the author there can be many layers of a folk text; it becomes a site for the criss-cross of several discourses. They exemplify what Barthes calls "the death of the author", allowing the readers ample freedom to appropriate them for their socio-cultural agendas.

The tales from *Kathasaritasagar* that engaged the attention of Mann and Karnad are parables mostly presented in the forms of riddles that engage the listeners/readers as much at the level of intellect as at the level of mystery. They excite the authors of our age to respond to the riddles intertextually and interculturally in an attempt to explore alternative answers to them. Folk tales, as I have already discussed, follow the pattern of stories-within-stories, stories branching out of stories, stories embedded in stories, running parallel and merging, spiralling, circulating in an internal rhythm. Karnad not only draws themes and motifs from this but also follows the folk narrative pattern. Karnad has admitted his indebtedness to Mann: "The central episode in the play – the story of Devadatta and Kapila – is based on a tale from *Vetalapanchabingashika* but I have drawn heavily on Thomas Mann's reworking of the tale in *The Transposed Heads* and am grateful to Mrs.Mann for permission to do so"(Qtd. Mahadevan, *Comparative Literature* 34). Though Mann has sensitised him to the subversive potentialities of the folk tale, provided him certain perspective, I may argue that it is his simultaneous engagement with Somadeva and Mann that gives Karnad enough freedom as well as direction to manipulate this tale for his own purpose.

Kathasaritasagar is a collection of frame stories, each story containing multiple short parables within it. One such frame story is that of King Vikramaditya, who is asked to fetch a corpse from a tree for a religious ritual. The corpse is however possessed by a being of supernatural power called *vetala*. As the king carries the corpse on his shoulder *vetala* recites a series of tales to the king, each with a riddle at the end. The story of the switching of heads is one of the twenty five riddle stories told by *vetala*. This narrates how a washerman Dhavala falls in love with Madanasundari, the beautiful daughter of another washerman, and marries her and enjoys the fruits of a happy marriage. Once Madanasundari's brother visits them and the three of them make a trip to the festival of Goddess Parvati. Dhavala enters the temple of Parvati, and in a fit of religious ecstasy beheads himself with the sacrificial sword as an offering to the goddess. Madanasundari's brother discovers the beheaded corpse, and in his pain and anguish beheads himself with the same sword. Madanasundari becomes anxious, when both men fail to return. She enters the temple and confronted by the horrible sight she too decides to commit suicide by hanging herself from vines. However the goddess, pleased with their devotion, stops her from committing suicide and allows her to bring the two men back to life by reattaching their heads to their bodies. Unfortunately, in her haste and confusion, Madanasundari puts her brother's head on her husband's body and vice versa. The story ends with a riddle, "Which of these mixed up persons is her husband?" The king replies that the one with the husband's head is her husband, because the head rules the limbs and personal identity depends on the head. In this story the parable is not the focus of the series, and like other parables it serves only to reveal the wisdom of King Vikramaditya. So the characters of the parable pale under the royal gaze. It affirms the superiority of the head over the body, the spirit over the flesh and the king over the common man. The story avoids any overt caste distinction. It asserts that a wife always embodies chastity and virtue and is rewarded by the goddess. While Mann uses the story to critique the ideology of pure Aryan identity and supremacy claimed by Nazi Germany, Karnad to question social inequality and foreground and project the marginalised - the folk, the lower class, and women.

Karnad's choiçe in reworking the parable from the *Kathasaritasagar* is quite consistent with his dramatic plan and programme of the exploration of the past for the need of the present that he has been carrying on. He has previously written two plays *Yayati* and *Tughlaq* based on Indian myth and history and continues this experiment in his plays *Nagamandala, Taldanda, Fire and Rain* that follow *Hayavadana*. In *Yayati* he has attempted a similar theme of the mixing up of the identities based on an episode from the *Mahabharata*, in which king Yayati exchanges his old age with the youth of his son. In his interpretation the dramatist gives a subversive role to Yayati's daughter-in-law Chitralekha, who confronts Yayati with a strange and shocking proposal that since he has taken her husband's youth he should accept her as his wife. In *Hayavadana* this theme of the confusion of identities is made more complex and extensive.

Karnad does not use the frame of Sanskrit theatre to bring the original Sanskrit tale to the stage but draws instead from folk theatre form such as *Yakshagana*. It is a Dravidian theatre for the lower classes enacted by lower class people paralleling the professional *natak* companies meant for the rich and urban elite. He himself has noted that he went with servants to the *Yakshagana* as a child (Dodiya 21). What interests him most is the subversive potential of the folk theatre form:

> The energy of the folk theatre comes from the fact that although it seems to uphold the traditional values it has the means of questioning these values making them literally stand on their head. The various conventions, the chorus, the masks, the seemingly unrelated comic episodes, the mixing of human and non-human worlds permit simultaneous presentation of alternative points of view, of alternative attitudes to central problems. (Dodiya, 34)

Apart from providing a means of critiquing the hegemonic order and various perspectives its open state performance mode for alternative approaches helps the dramatist break the fourth wall that separates the stage from the audience and subvert the close alienated bourgeois world represented by the self-contained box-office proscenium stage.

The play opens with an invocation of Lord Ganesh, the elephant-headed god, which is an introductory ritual in a Hindu ceremony or celebration. This involves the audience at a community— participatory level and disrupts the splendid isolationism of illusionistic theatre mode. It suggests *darshan* which means 'sight' that leads to 'insight' implying deeper involvement of the spectators. This also introduces the central theme of the conflict between the head and the body. If indeed the head rules the body, Ganesh should have been like an elephant, which according to folk belief is considered the most foolish of all animals. Here the head takes on the identity of the body, which originally belonged to Ganesh. Again how does the god made of the dirt of Parvati and with a head replaced by Shiva, as the myth says, signify the idea of harmony and perfection? This is a paradox that invests the ordinary with the extraordinary, the common with the uncommon, the banal with the mysterious. This myth of Ganesh has another significance. It presents a complex dialectic of discursive erasure and cultural appropriation. Ganesh, it has been pointed out, was initially a pre-Vedic deity, and later on has been appropriated by the mainstream Hinduism resulting in the erasure of his pre-Aryan tribal origin from discourses. Many scholars have suggested the tribal origins of such many Hindu Gods—Narasimha (Lion Man), Varaha (Boar-Man), and Jagannath (See *The Cult of Jagannath*.. Eds. Eschmann, et al., 1978). Thus, this introductory ritual points to the traces of the primitive, the tribal, the subtext of the other in our culture, that we tend to ignore but the playwright wants to excavate.

One significant departure from Mann's version in *Hayavadana* is the addition of a frame story of Hayavadana (horseman). As Bhagavata, who combines the roles of the director and the stage manager, starts narrating the story of Devadatta and Kapila, a character called Actor representing the *Yakshagana* actor enters the stage. He reports that when he was trying to piss at the roadside he was warned by a horse-headed man not to commit that nuisance on the main road. Actor's encounter with the horseman has several implications. First, the fact that the man with a horse-head is endowed with civic sense which Actor, a fully human being, lacks undermines the supposed superiority of head over body, even of human over non-human. Second, Hayavadana, who, as he narrates, later on to Bhagavata, has already visited many places of pilgrimage of great national and mythological significance, Banares, Allahabad, Dwaraka, etc., all over India and has studied "the social life of Nations—Civics, Politics, Patriotism, Nationalism, Indianisation, the Socialist Pattern of Society"—with the purpose of becoming completely human, has perhaps been infected with high elitism that scorns folk manners (*Modern Indian Drama*, 263). The words like 'Nation', 'Civics', 'Politics', 'Patriotism', 'Nationalism', 'Indianisation', 'Socialist Pattern of

Society' written with capital letters in the beginning suggest elitist nationalism or the totalitarian nationalist discourse that distorts the social polity by ignoring the interests and aspirations of community states. Hayavadana's failure to become complete, inspite of all these high religious and academic pursuits, is the evidence of the inadequacy of such national imaginary. The anachronism that a pre-modern character talks about modern discourses posits the story in the contemporary context.

Bhagavata advises Hayavadana to visit the temple of Kali on Mount Chitrakoot in a jungle worshipped by the tribal folk suggesting that the involvement with the local, with the folk can be the basis for true nationalism and self-realisation. Any scheme of national imaginary, it implies, must include and acknowledge various imagined nations or community states. Kali, an ungodly goddess, ugly, grotesque and terrifying stands for the stark concrete physicality that can act as a counter to abstract spirituality and as a cure for the morbid obsession with the head. Kali is more masculine than feminine, and is represented as standing above Shiva with a garland of severed heads around her neck; this points to the reversal of the social, sexual, gender hierarchy, that the play is working towards. The transformation of Parvati of Somadeva's tale to Kali in Karnad's marks the changed situation of the empowerment of women, and is significantly related to the cult of Shakti in the matriarchal society of the pre-Aryans/tribals.

The story of the origin of Hayavadana gives an interesting and suggestive account of the situation of woman. Hayavadana's mother is a beautiful princess, who, in a *swayamvar* (a ceremony in which a princess is allowed to choose her bridegroom), instead of choosing one of the handsome princes, who have assembled for her hands, chooses a stallion. It marks, I can argue, a radical revolt against the very tradition of *swayamvar*, that has become more a show of feudal authority and patriarchal power than a genuine expression of desire to give freedom to women, particularly when the choice is limited to only those royal personages selected and invited by the king- father, not open to all. The princes gathered have often to prove their prowess to win the hands of the princess thus reducing woman to a prize, a commodity to be won and owned. The role of father as a feudal lord accentuates the position of woman as a subordinate class. This half-hearted attempt to meet woman's desire for freedom further alienates woman. The princess's intuitive perception of the extra-animalic in the animal is proved later on by the metamorphosis of the stallion into a gandharva, a divine minstrel. Her instinct and intuition proves superior to the diabolic intellect of her father. When the gandharva, after being released from curse, asks her to accompany him to heaven, she refuses to do so and asks him instead to return to the animalic form, because she suspects this act as another patriarchal design, she has been so scared of. Her suspicion becomes true when gandharva in his masculine fury curses her to be a horse and leaves her.

Distinct caste and racial distinctions are introduced into Karnad's tale as in Mann's version. The representations of Devadatta, a brahmin, on the stage as a slender and delicate looking person wearing a pale coloured mask and of Kapila, a blacksmith, as a well-built person wearing a dark mask follows the traditional assumption of colour as the marker of caste and of brahmin standing for the head and other castes for other limbs. Padmini, the daughter of a trader, belongs to an intermediate caste. Her name refers to the Padmini type, categorised by Vatsayan, an ancient sage and scholar as the best of the six types of women. She is expected to be docile, graceful and faithful to be adored by men. The play begins with these hegemonic constructions and moves gradually pulling them down.

In the beginning, I may point out, Padmini has not chosen her husband; she has rather been chosen by Devadatta and approached by Kapila on Devadatta's behalf, not very much unlike the princess, Hayavadana's mother, whose freedom was a travesty of freedom. But Padmini's marriage to Devadatta, instead of her belonging to a lower caste, refutes the brahminic ideology of purity. She is interpreted by Bhagavata and the female chorus as a Yogini, a diabolically attractive woman. This is opposite of Padmini type and can be an extension of the image of Kali, which provides a frame of reference for subversion in the play:

Bhagavata (sings): They forgot themselves and took off their bodies. And she took the laughing heads, but held these high, so the pouring blood bathed her, coloured her red, then she danced around and sang.

Female chorus (sings): The blood pours into the earth and a song branches out in the sky. (265)

This presents a vision of the powerful feminine force to which men have to surrender for sweetness and harmony in the world. Devadatta and Kapila, we find are complementary as well as contrasting characters. Devadatta, a learned pundit, is supposed to stand for the head but his knowledge is bookish and has little relation with life and reality. He describes Padmini parroting old similes and images, lines quoted from Kalidas and others. He is imitative, not creative. On the contrary, Kapila, a blacksmith, is active, energetic and courageous—his driving bullock cart, climbing the tree, plucking flowers, swimming and wrestling display the wondrous magic of the body. Padmini has been in fact wooed by Kapila on behalf of Devadatta, who loves but lacks the courage to express his love. The sight of Kapila nimbly and skilfully climbing the tree to bring her the Fortunate Lady flowers moves Padmini to the enchanting poetry of body:

> And what the ethereal shape! Such a broad back like an ocean with muscles rippling across it and then that small, feminine waist which looks so helpless. (278)

She finds in his body her ideal of beauty, the harmonious combination of the ethereal and the concrete, the masculine and the feminine, the divine and the animalic. He is a "celestial hunter being reborn as a hunter. How his body sways, his limbs curve—it's a dance almost" (239). The allusion is to Lord Shiva descending on earth for love-sports with Parvati, who takes the shape of a huntress. Kapila, perceived as a combination of the divine and the animalic, is linked to Gandharva-as-stallion in the frame story. His description of the Fortunate Lady flower of married woman is a representation of folk imagination:

> Because it has all the marks of marriage a woman puts on. The yellow on the petals—then that red round patch at the bottom of petals—like the parting of your hair—They—

> when... Oh yes hear, near the stem a row of black dots like a necklace of black beads—(279).

He combines sense of details with abstract imagination. Opposed to the elitist poet Devadatta he is a folk poet, a poet of body and nature.

At the centre of the play is the transposition of heads. Padmini on the instruction of Kali, in haste and confusion, joins Devadatta's head to Kapila's body. Her attraction for Kapila's body has certainly turned into an unconscious desire that moves the action to such confusion. The unconscious here subverts the conscious. Though apparently an inadvertent action it appears she has willed this transposition. Kali is merely the external manifestation of her powerful diabolic unconscious. Padmini has earlier been described as a *Yogini,* a tantric figure by Bhagavata preparing us for such a role of hers, to which Devadatta and Kapila have to surrender. It is her strong erotic power, her intense imaginative participation with the vital forces of life that bring about such a miraculous change, which can only be expressed through spirituo-mystical occurrences. The primitive tantric cult of a body mystique subverts the other-worldly soul-centred brahminic ideology. It undermines the masculine supremacy too. The mixing up of a brahmin and a blacksmith negates the brahminic ideology of purity. This Kali image of Padmini subverts the stereo-typification of woman, best represented by the Padmini type as graceful, docile and faithful. She is like Mann's Sita, who in his version turns out to be a parody of mythical Sita, deconstructs the notion of chastity used as an instrument of patriarchal control.

Padmini at last accepts the-Devdatta- head- and- the -Kapila-body as her husband. Not satisfied with the answer of Vikramaditya, Karnad follows Mann in extending the story. In the play Vikramaditya is replaced by a rishi. The dominant culture of the head starts gradually asserting through its manipulatory rationality and hegemonic mysticism. In course of time Devadatta and Kapila are back to their former selves. Again Padmini has to confront the arid intellectuality of Devadatta and the physical vitality of Kapila.

Another folk form used here as an expressionistic device in reporting the changes taking place in Devadatta and the inner turmoil of Padmini is that of puppet form. The earthy humour and satire with which the puppets speak about Devadatta, Padmini and their child makes light of the victory of the head over the body. Related to the puppet form is another folk form lullaby that Padmini sings to her son singing of a handsome horse–rider. She dreams of a spiritually charged healthy body. At the end Padmini meets Kapila in the forest and stays with him and Devadatta goes in search of her. Devadatta and Kapila start fighting against each other for possession of Padmini. The stage instruction says:

> Devadatta and Kapila, at the end, have to wage the final battle over Padmini:
>
> The fight is stylised like a dance. Their swords don't touch. Even Padmini's reaction is like a dance. (313)

They all join the dance of life and death. The death of Devadatta and Kapila is a rhythmic movement into another life, as they earlier died into their changed lives and identities. That brahmin Devadatta, known for his timidity, ultimately wields a sword and fights for his love is his recognition of the claims of the body. Bhagavata in the play describes the sword fight as a cockfight, a folk pastime that the tribal people indulge in and enjoy. The tribal discourse is used here to ridicule any attempt to find a final and neat resolution of the conflicts and to point to the fundamental irresolution at the heart of everything. This is what Homi Bhabha calls "lived perplexity". The tribal belief and practice of enshrining the dead ancestors as a part of their environment is the acceptance of death as a part of the eternal pattern. This provides a perspective to this conflictual situation.

Padmini's self-immolation is not exactly an act of sati. The song of the chorus singing of her journey in a decorated palanquin of sandalwood, I can point out, is rather a celebration of the Shakti, who has fought against bondages. Anand Mahadevan appropriately states, "this change of focus from abstract masculine thought to concrete feminine action is responsible for the subversion of the traditional values of the probable in these works" (Comparative *Literature* 29). She acts out her inner impulses, "the thick yearning of the many petalled many flowered lantana" (315). She deconstructs the Padmini type that is a patriarchal attempt to pigeon-hole woman into a static situation, into a fixed entity, and eventually herself turns it into a padmini, a lotus, "a many-petalled many-flowered lantana." Thus Padmini is invested with ambiguous significances; one significance deconstructs the other; while the former is foregrounded the latter is backgrounded. She imaginatively splits her lover into multiple selves and merges them and fashions out multiple identities. She is an artist of life, who dissipates and combines life-realities into beautiful patterns. Bhagavata indicates she has turned into "a full blossomed, tree of the Fortunate Lady" (314) whose flowers she once longed for. But the play does not give any assurance of her attaining complete selfhood; it is a dance, a game and a continuing process of subversion and reconstruction.

Hayavadana of the story turns into a horse, for while praying to Kali he fails to ask to make him "complete man" but instead only asks to make him "complete". This may be due to his deep inward disaffection with human society. This process of de-evolution which is a voluntary act in case of the princess and an expression of the unconscious desire in case of her son, I may point out, is a repudiation of the grand narrative of the progressive evolution as depicted in the narrative of *Dashavatar* or Ten Incarnations. The ten incarnations of Lord Vishnu as presented in our mythology refer to different shapes that Vishnu had to take to kill demons that terrorised the earth and the heaven. They are the fish, the tortoise, the boar, the lion-man, the dwarf, then Rama, Parashurama, Krishna, Buddha and Kalki. This shows the gradual evolution of life from unicellular organism to multi-cellular animal, man. This play dramatises a radical decentring that deconstructs the notion of man as spirit, seen at the centre as a fiction, or a construct.

All these situations of metamorphosis of the princes and Hayavadana into horses, the gandharva in the form of a stallion, the transposition of heads, the images of Ganesh and Kali appear grotesque. They can be interpreted as a means of bringing the high, the abstract, the hollow elitists down to the material and physical level. This can be explained with the help of Mikhail Bakhtin's concept of grotesque realism. For Bakhtin's grotesque realism celebrates "the material bodily principle," and depicts "degradation, that is the lowering of all that is high, spiritual, ideal, abstract, it is a transfer to the material level, to the sphere of earth and body in their indissoluble unity" (*Rabelais and His World* 19-20). This explains the transposition of heads that brings Devadatta down to the physical and Padmini's search for the vital, the bodily, and the earthly. Divine artists gandharvas are usually cursed to be born as animals because of their violation of rhythm during their performance in the court of Lord Indra and this failure is also due to their loss of contact with the earthly and the physical. Hence there is the need for renewing their contact with reality for which they are sent to the earth. The *Yakshagana* style, the puppet form, the cockfight are all the means of getting the abstract spirituality entangled in the physical and the material.

The two plots meet, when Hayavadana, now tuned into a horse, and Padmini's child brought up by the hunters meet in the presence of Bhagavata. The horse laughs and sings. Because of his hesitation and his inability to completely speak out his wish some human trace remains with him. The boy, on the other hand does not speak, cry or smile. Actor comments on the boy. "When he grows up he should make a good theatre critic" (317). It means he would grow into a serious and grave person. This is a satirical reflection on the present-day theatre critics, who are so elitist that they turn their grave sophisticated nose away from any folk stuff.

Karnad in the play suggests not only a new theatrical mode but also a critical perspective for the evaluation of contemporary theatre. The boy is to be sent to his grandfather Vidyasagar to complete his education according to the expressed wish of his mother. He has been trained in the culture of body—sports and martial art by the hunters in the jungle and needs the training of the mind. The horse then sings the national anthem – this fact is a critique on singing the national anthem without realising its significance. Its significance lies in the celebration of the vital plurality of India, the recognition of the multicultural identities, not in the monolithic unitary nationalism. Even the animals is not to be excluded from the national imaginary. The laughing horse provokes the mute boy to laugh and the boy's laughter cures the horse of his human voice. This is another kind of exchange or transposition that brings them back to their respective social folds. The boy rides the horse away into the city. This image of the horse-rider has been envisioned by Padmini when she has sung a lullaby earlier to her son. This is a vision of a folk hero who learns to acknowledge and control instinct and passion, recognise and transcend differences. It is a vision of the harmony between soul and body, man and animal, man and woman and high class/caste and low class/caste.

This epilogue of the play is a song of benediction, a concluding prayer to Ganesh. The fourth wall of the stage ruptured from time to time is finally broken as Padmini, Devadatta and Kapila step forward to join Bhagavata and the chorus in the prayer. This is quite in conformity with the folk theatre mode; this is what Brecht emphasises—the self-conscious acting as an epic theatre device that views actors separate from characters they interpret on the stage. This folk theatre type refutes the notion of an enclosed stage space used by elitist dramatists to inflict their ideologies on passive audience. It extends to include the auditorium to provide the spectators with scope and perspectives for judging the play and symbolically the whole world with its variety and diversity. Karnad has pointed out the use of the two types of scenes in the post-independence India drama – "shallow" and "deep scenes" (Dodiya 27). "Shallow" scenes primarily deal with lower classes, and are humorous interludes between serious "deep" scenes involving rich surroundings and kings and courtiers. *Yakshagana* has only one plane of action and lacks class-conscious differentiation. When he was writing *Tughlaq* he found "the shallow scenes bulging with an energy hard to control" (Dodiya 28). In *Hayavadana* that follows it "shallow" scenes swallow "deep scene" as Mahadevan has pointed out (37). The troubling subtext becomes the text. *Hayavadana* presents, to quote Bakhtin, a situation of carnival, in which "life turned inside out", "which is a minimally ritualised antiritual, a festive celebration of the other" *(Dostoevsky's Poetics,* 122*)*.

KARNAD'S *NAGAMANDALA*

In *Nagamandala* Karnad turned to the folklore of Karnataka – the folktale lived and sustained by the rural folk of Karnataka—to construct a regional discourse emblematic of cultural diversity opposed to totalitarian concept of nationalism. He uses here a fantastic situation of the love between a woman and a cobra to critique the unequal oppressive relationship between man and woman in our patriarchal society and also to critique, in a subtle manner, class-caste distinction. Correspondingly the diegetic and fantastic elements found plenty in folktales and folk beliefs are exploited to subvert the dominant realistic trend. Diegesis (narration) and fantasy are used in the play to support and qualify each other in dramatic framework.

The setting of *Nagamandala* is the inner sanctum of a ruined temple on a moonlit night. The idol is broken and the presiding deity cannot be identified. But in *Hayavadana* the temple, where crucial action of the play takes place, is a temple of Goddess Kali, who being associated with the graveyard, is considered originally as the goddess of low caste people, later on appropriated by the mainstream religion. A fierce-looking blackgoddess with a protruding tongue, wearing garlands of severed heads and hands, stands for the desirable disorder. Kali as an ungodly goddess is appropriately invoked upon to witness the dismemberment of body and subsequent body-head or body-soul and caste-class confusion. Here in *Nagamandala* the ruined temple and broken idol indicate the void, absence, lack or what we may call disappearance of "metanarrative" which is represented by the traditional brahminic order (Lyotard 1984:XXIV).. Moonlight suggests desire for alternatives and possibilities of filling up the void.

The character, who introduces the play, is identified as Man, who is a fictional representation of the playwright. He acts as a frame- narrator serving the function of a prologue. Discontented with well-made plays written in imitation of western Style, Man has been in search of alternative paradigms. The namelessness of the narrator Man is not simply a representation of any modern author facing the crisis of expression or of cultural representation but signifies death of the author. Rolland Barthes has explained this negation of the author by interpreting the text as "a tissue, a quotation drawn from the innumerable centres of culture" (*Modern Criticism and Theory*, 1998: 170). Hence not Man but a character called Story is the generative narrator – the narrator who generates the story, which implies the notion of the text generating texts, texts embedded in the texts. Story is, in a sense, Man in an intertextual space. This is true of folk tales, most of which, as I have suggested earlier while discussing *Hayavadana*, are authorless and follow the pattern of stories branching out, stories embedded in stories, running parallel and merging, spiraling, circulating in an internal rhythm. These devices of narrator in a drama, associated with Brechtian alienation effect and of story-within-story identified with Pirandelian meta-theatre are rather rediscovered/located by Karnad in Indian folk tradition. Thus Karnad has chosen a style that disrupts the dominant colonial discourse and also attempts to appropriate certain relevant elements of the Western discourse.

A symbolic-allegorical approach is to be adopted to the play, because in it non-human characters like flames, Story, King Cobra play as important roles as human characters. Man apprehends his death, as warned by a mendicant, if he fails to keep awake that night. It is not death in performance that he has staged many a time but the death of the author within that troubles him. He feels the exhaustion of inner resources, the void within that extends to the void without. A mendicant in an Indian society is a wandering holy man, a repository of folk wisdom, who sings *Puranas* and folk songs, predicts the future and sometimes gives or prescribes herbal cures and is believed to know magic. Thus he is a culture figure, who wants to open Man's eyes to his cultural past, his present sickness and future alternatives. He says to him:

> You have written plays. You have staged them. You have caused so many good people, who came trusting you, to fall asleep twisted in miserable chairs, that all that abused mass of sleep has turned against you and become the curse of Death. (*Nagamandala* 2)

The traditional plays that Man, the playwright, has written and staged, have administered people doses of sentiment and entertainment and made people sleepy, dormant and passive, killed the initiative and creativity of the audience, made them marginalised, "the other" and in a sense caused their death. To atone this, the mendicant asks Man to keep awake and to keep a kind of holy-vigil. This presupposes that he has symbolically slept away all the nights allowing himself to become a passive channel for transmission of dominant ideologies to the audience and thereby obstructing latter's thinking power. This also literally alludes to the fact that he has been more exposed to and has all along practised proscenium theatre, which is usually staged in the evenings watched mainly by urban elite class, but he has not paid any attention to the folk theatres like *Yakshagana*, which are staged all through the night mostly enjoyed by the rural folk. The opening monologue, is a non-dramatic narrative which, after Bakhtin, can be called interior dialogue that man carries on with himself, with suppressed social structures and forms preserved in the unconscious. It implies that he is to keep awake to other alternatives, and suppressed folk voices.

Eastern folk tales have had their origin in man's attempt to soothe troubled minds and give guidance to confused minds as we find in cases of *Panchatantra*, in which Vishnu Sharma teaches the unruly princes through tales. They are used to circumvent death as Laila uses tales to save herself in *Tales from Arabian Nights.* Also they are used as a means of release from curse as in case of *Kathasaritasagar*, in which Gunadhya, cursed by Lord Shiv for secretly listening to the tales told to Parvati, had to tell stories to people for his redemption from the curse. Man, the author in *Nagamandala*, who is in a troubled mind in the face of the crisis of expression and carries the curse of the audience/people, turns to folk forms for his redemption. The play is based on two folk tales from Karnataka which, Girish Karnad has stated in his preface, he heard from poet A.K. Ramanujan several years ago. One is the tale of Story, and ensconced within this is the tale of the love between a woman and King Cobra. The tale told by Story may be a fantasy of Man, as it enacts man's imagined encounter with the significances and relevances of folk culture in the present context. This reflects the ambivalence of the subject position of man—he is subjected to cultural forces and his role as an initiator of change is also the construct of the cultural forces.

The first fantastic scene in the play is that of flames "just lamp flames, on their own floating in the air! Is that even possible?" (*Naga*-2). Man expresses 'hesitation', hesitation between reality and fantasy, between realistic frame and the fantastic content, which according to Todorov is a feature of literary fantasy (Qtd. Jackson, 1981: 28). This episode is based on the folk belief that during nights after people sleep putting out lamps, the flames of the lamps gather at the village temple and gossip. The representation of flames as timid women in contrast to the traditional representation of fire as ferocious masculine god of fire (Agni in Hindu mythology) indicates the playwright's attempt to focus on domestic feminine situation. The conversation among the flames throws up comic details about queer nature of the masters of houses. A skinflint master is miserly about spending money on oil and does not trust his wife with money and goes to bed early; one had kept the light burning to keep vigil over his ailing mother but turned off light early on the day of his mother's death to go to bed to enjoy his wife; another sexually perverse husband, wants to have sex with his wife under the glare of light as if eating her up limb by limb. These small details tell one story of patriarchal domination - economic and sexual. New Flame, who arrives last tells a tale of fantasy. When her mistress, an old woman, after finishing her work, entered her bedroom she saw a young woman dressed in a red sari step out of the room; when she questioned her husband, her husband expressed his ignorance. New Flame explains this mystery. His mistress knew a story and a song but kept them to herself, never told the story, nor sang the song, and they were choked inside her. That afternoon as the old woman took her usual nap after lunch, opened her mouth snoring, the story and the song jumped out and hid in the attic. The story took the form of a young woman and the song became a sari; that young woman, Story-and-Song, stepped out, just as the old woman was coming in. This tale read along with other three tales of flames points to the silencing of the voices of women, and more specifically of the art of storytelling, the most powerful and moving medium available to women for self-expression and self-assertion. That flames are chosen to tell the plight of women expresses one redeeming feature that in spite of the suffering women are aware of their suffering, as flames stand for awareness. One significant point that emerges here is the fact that in spite of the storyteller the story gets told, "so if you try to gag one story another happens" (*Naga* 4). Story survives the suppression of patriarchy and the onslaught of urbanisation and technology. Story here becomes the storyteller implying that the story generates stories, branching out into stories or continuing and sustaining in an intertextual manner.

Man jumps up to listen to this story to keep awake and to be released from the curses of audience for having kept them under the anaesthesia of dominant ideologies and traditional entertainment and to ward off death. In Brihat's *Kathasaritasagar* Gunadhya tells stories to save himself, the story teller, not the listener, from curse; so also in the Arabian tales, Laila tells story to save herself from death. Here in *Nagamandala* there is a reversal; it is the listener who is to be kept awake, to be saved from death and the curses of the audience. He is a spectator/listener to be saved from dullness and passivity that he has heaped on his audience. Man, in order to survive is urged upon to turn into a storyteller like Gunadhya and pass the story on. But Man's hesitation about this responsibility is expressive of the uncertainty about any new experimentation. Keeping awake in this context means overcoming the amnesia that time piles upon people's psyche, and particularly the cultural amnesia produced by years of colonialism, and suggests regaining and reshaping of memory.

The story of *Nagamandala* told by Story is the story of a woman, Rani's use of all the resources available to her to confront patriarchal oppression. Every day Apanna leaves his wife Rani locked up inside his house, goes out, spends his night with a concubine, returns next day for lunch and again goes out. When she questions him he says, "Look, I don't like idle chatter. Don't question me. Do as you are told and you won't be punished" (*Naga* 7). Male supremacist ideology sanctioned by our culture results in the deprivation and loss for women. This loss and emptiness Rani counters with her fantasies of being transported by an eagle beyond the seven seas and the seven isles to a tree of emeralds in a magic garden on the seventh island, where she is kissed and embraced by her parents, of being wooed by a prince in the guise of a stag: "In the morning a stag with golden antlers comes to the door. He calls out to Rani. She refuses to go "I am not a stag" he explains, "I am a prince ..." (*Naga* 7). Shape-shifting which is the central motif of this play is suggested here as an abstract dream.

Tales of love-making between humans and non-humans, of supernatural and even human characters magically changing their shapes, and of half human half animalic forms are found in plenty in eastern and western mythologies and folk tales. In *Hayavadana,* as we have already observed, Karnad has used a story of the marriage between a princess and a stallion and the birth of a horse-headed man, the transposition of heads and bodies of two persons to explore the mysterious composition of selfhood and politics of identity involved. The element of magic present in the fantasy–narration of Rani finds dramatic enactment, when blind woman Kurudavva, a friend of Apanna's mother, carried by her son Kapanna comes to the window of Rani's house. Moved by her tale of woe, she offers to help her with magic roots whose paste, if administered to her husband, will make him submissive. That a blind woman is presented as a magic woman suggests a powerful inner vision developed through the folk wisdom. Her son Kapanna, who is fair but is paradoxically called Kapanna, (Kapanna means an inhabitant of darkness), indicates her and his association with dark mysteries of magic used for people's well being. Those magic roots, as described by Kurudavva, are kept well-wrapped in a piece of paper in a coconut shell inside a wooden box in a tightly tied bundle of cloth kept a tin trunk inside in a shelf behind the pillar in her house. This is related to Rani's fantasy of being transported beyond seven seas and seven isles. The folk tale motif of journey through multiple protective and dangerous layers to get at the secret is used here to convey an entangled and compounded sense of secrecy, mystery, power and horror that marks women's struggle at multiple levels against deeply-entrenched patriarchy. Rani first fails with the shorter piece of root. But when she pours the paste of the longer piece of root into the curry meant for Apanna, the curry turns red blood. This confuses and frightens Rani as Apanna might notice this or this might harm him. As Apanna arrives, then, Story prompts her, "Rani, put it in the anthill" (17). Story, this shows, is an external narrator as well as an externalisation of a part of Rani's self. As she pours out that curry there King Cobra lifts its head hissing out of the anthill. At the dead of night, Story relates, cobra enters the house through the drain of the bathroom, takes the form of Apanna and enters Rani's bedroom.

Naga in the guise of Apanna is Apanna in the role of a soft, sweet and adoring lover completely different from Apanna, a rough, rude and aggressive husband. This magical transformation, I would like to state, is effected through the arousal of vital energy and erotic power (that snake stands for) largely brought about by Rani's exercise of feminine charm and power gifted to her by folk wisdom, deeply rooted in folk tradition as represented by the magic roots. Added to it is the folk belief and practice of taming snakes through magic. The snake, as it adorns the head of Lord Shiva represented by phallus-like stone, stands for procreative force. And mandala is a term from magic signifying charmed circle, which can cast spell.

The entire game of love between Naga and Rani is presented through images of love between male and female cobras depicting variety and intensity of lovemaking. It is very relevant to mention here that cobras are known for their strong passionate love-making. The love-dance of male and female cobras entertwined with each other, their playful love-chase, their longing and pining for each other are sights often seen in Indian countryside. "Now, don't be silly. I am not a mongoose or a hawk that you should be so afraid of me ...What beautiful, long hair! Like dark black snake princess", Naga pleads with Rani *(21)*. In the beginning of the play the comparison of the tresses of Rani to snakes has foreshadowed her possible role as a female cobra in the game of love at this stage.

Rani, who in the beginning imagines herself being wooed by a prince in the guise of a stag with golden antler, finds herself being wooed by a cobra in the shape of a man – the former being a man in the form of an animal, the latter an animal in the form of a man. While the former is a dream of a tender quiescent emotion of love, the latter is an enactment of strong erotic passion. This love between human and snake like that that between Arjuna and Snake Princess Ulupi, between Bhima and Snake Princess Nagabala romantically celebrated in the *Mahabharata* is common in our myths preserved in collective unconscious, that lends credibility and comprehensibility to the story.

In the daytime Apanna, the husband, appears. Seeing distaste and indifference in Apanna's face Rani is terribly confused and thinks the last night's experience might be a dream. In the night Naga returns and says, "It is not a dream. I am not a figment of your imagination either. I am here, I am sitting in front of you. Touch me" (22). It is both reality and dream. Rani confronts him: "You talk so nicely at night. But during the day I only have to open my mouth and you hiss like a ...stupid snake" (22). In the night, not in the daytime, the snake appears but in the daytime Apanna behaves like a snake. It is a snake all the time. In the night Rani imagines herself as a bird stupefied by the hypnotic gaze of a snake. Two dimensions of the snake image – violent, aggressive and irrational on the one hand, quiet, loving and enchanting on the other – refer to the two aspects of man. One night Rani is horrified to see in the mirror the image of a snake, which, in fact, is the reflection of Naga sitting behind her. The mirror gives the objective picture of the snake. The mirror image may be a reflection of Rani's conceptualisation and internalisation of the image of her lover as seductive, secretive and mysterious as a snake. Their love-making is elemental, animalic and earthy like that of snake-lovers; this is presented in a song that depicts that the female cobra begins to smell like the wet earth; and stung by her smell the king cobra starts searching for his queen. Flames, then, sing and dance out the climax of love. They perform a choric function through narration and mimesis. Apanna's relationship with the concubine points to coarse vulgar sexuality different from loving elegant companionship between Rani and Naga.

A dog and a mongoose kept by Apanna to keep watch over the house stand for social and cultural restraints, with which men try to control and regulate sexuality, and control women. This leads to an aggressive form of the wounded sexuality. Naga is eventually injured fighting against them and turns sexually aggressive. Kurudavva makes a second visit to her. She then feels the lock outside the house and Kapanna reports that Rani is inside. They see the cobra go out and Rani through the window-crack tells that she is happy and her husband has just gone out, but they don't see the lock open. Their perplexity is confounded, when they turn and see Apanna coming from outside. This interplay between reality and fantasy can only be explained as revelatory of the incomprehensible, elusive and mysterious nature of love and lovers' ways akin to supernatural occurrences.

There is a parallel and complementary tale of Kapanna's vision of his love for Yakshini (one of divine maidens in charge of treasures working under the direction of Lord Kuber, the God of wealth). While Rani is in love with someone from the nether world, Kapanna is in love with a maid from the upper world. While the former is enacted, the latter is reported. This earth as the meeting ground of the supernatural, the human and the animalic points to the coexistence of these three elements in man. These episodes are, in a sense, dramatisaticn of the intercourse between these three levels going on in the self of man.

The two roles of husband and lover kept so meticulously separate from each other tend to get mixed up and threaten each other. Pregnancy complicates and problematises Rani's subject position. It is she who starts the erotic game, transforms a dull indifferent man to a lover skilful in all erotic arts, lends their love some magical charm; but in course of the game she finds herself subjugated. Rani eventually finds no basic difference between the two roles – her lover Naga in the night time and her husband Apanna in the day time, belong to the same patriarchy which justifies itself in terrorising women into submission. These two identities are only the postures that she questions:

> But day or right one motto does not change. Don't ask questions. Do as I tell you. *(32)*

She has gained her night to have free and joyous love, control her sexuality, reclaims her body but confronts all forms of patriarchal power. Maternity gives Rani added strength, a sense of superiority, for she realises that she is not one, she is two and she has another role and responsibility awaiting her. This third role not only threatens the existence of the other two roles but also disturbs the balance between the two maintained so far. The lover addicted to love is not prepared to welcome a child and the husband plunged in worldly pursuit has forgotten the other erotic self.

The crucial situation occurs when Naga is face to face with Apanna, as the former is leaving and the latter is coming in:

> They both freeze. The lights change sharply from night to mid-day. In a flash, Naga becomes Apanna. Pushes her to the floor and kicks her. (33)

This establishes the identity between and inseparability of Naga and Apanna. Apanna's subsequent charge of adultery against his wife is a charge against his strange mysterious erotic self, which he is not able to recognise from the vantage point of the dull mechanical day-to-day life. Mired in routine life, trapped in the carnal sexuality provided by his relationship with a whore he can't raise himself to that level of emotion and imagination required for recognising the vitalised love. Only in the night his heart is on fire and his imagination runs riot. Subsequently Apanna complains against his wife before village elders who represent patriarchal structure, which only questions female transgression but ignores male transgression and even considers the latter as a male privilege.

Rani will have to undertake some ordeals like holding a red hot iron to prove her chastity. Some kind of miracle, the magic of mind and heart, a leap in imagination is required to reconcile the opposites. When the lover Naga advises Rani to undertake snake ordeal—to swear by putting her hand on the hood of a cobra, Naga appears different from his earlier image. He is shorn off his false patriarchal ego and surrenders to the maternal image of Rani. The public show of punishment, as Foucault has argued, is to ensure the visibility of punishment that would terrorise others into submission and help perpetuate the hegemony of the dominant class (*Discipline and Punish*, 1979: 197). The reversal of such an all-pervasive, long-sustained, deeply-entrenched design can only be possible through a strong determined stand, an intense imaginative participation in the vital life, which can be equated with a miracle. Rani thus pulls the cobra out of the anthill and swears:

> Yes, my husband and this King Cobra. Except for these two, I have not touched any one of the male sex. Nor have I allowed any other male to touch me. If I lie let the cobra bite me. (439)

It is a swearing by the source of vital energy, which brings about a transformation. The cobra then comes out and hangs around her neck like a garland, which signifies the taming of the primordial forces of life and projects her role of a snake charmer. Before villagers she is transformed into a divine being, a goddess who subsumes all the images of woman. The deification of woman, at this stage, is not another patriarchal ideology of keeping woman immobile and static by pigeonholing her to certain fixed image or concept but it marks the male recognition of the female power. She becomes a combination of a tantric woman and a goddess.

The parallel and complementary story of the love between Kapanna and Yakshini reaches its climax, when Kurudavva suddenly arrives at the gathering of villagers and reports that her son is missing and he might have run away with that Yakshini. Human and non-human relationship is extended to include man and angel relationship and this is significantly related to Rani's symbolic metamorphosis into a goddess. We can very well infer from this that Yakhini is a part of Rani, Kapanna is a simple and innocent side of the complex Apanna. Of these two stories one is enacted the other one is reported. Kurudavva, whose magic is indirectly responsible for this imbroglio involving Rani, ironically finds herself trapped in an imbroglio of a similar type. This demonstrates the magic of all magics – the mystery of life that entangles all.

Rani, at the end, gets a devoted husband, leads a happy life, lives her own life, refuses to be an object of man's project. Apanna's concubine, who was present at the ordeal, becomes her servant, which implies that vulgar wanton sexuality is brought under control. Rani's story of transformation charts out a course from a timid frightened village girl through the stages of elegant erotic love and wild sexuality in to a self-confident mother figure and ultimately to a goddess/enchantress figure—a woman possessing transcendent love and power that includes and transcends all the possible roles of wife, mother and mistress.

The ending of the play raises many questions and issues that are debated between Story and Man to provide alternative perspectives to the audience in formulating their responses. There is no closure to the play; the play remains open with many alternatives and possibilities. Can Apanna be happy, though he knows fully well that he has not slept with Rani? How can Rani be contented, when she will find Apanna's lovemaking different from Naga's lovemaking? These questions can be answered with the help of the notion that man's identity is not an immutable entity but a changing one; man is a bundle of reflections, a multiple of performances in changing relational contexts. So love-making varies from time to time corresponding to differing identities and changing relational contexts, and varying erotic moods and modes. The myriad forms and shades of love that lovers together explore and enact account for its strangeness vary and mystery.

In response to the question regarding the fate of King Cobra an alternative ending is suggested through narration and enactment. One night Naga pays a visit to Rani, and is driven to madness and anguish to see her with Apanna. He enters into her tresses and makes love to them. "Naga ties a tress into a noose and places it around his neck", narrates Story (43). When Rani feels uncomfortable and finds it difficult to comb her hair, Apanna combs her hair and the cobra falls dead. This is suggestive of the memory of earlier love, whose spell needs to be broken for life to move on and a loving and caring husband alone can help break this spell. This symbolises the breakdown of the wall of separation between the roles of the lover and the husband and man's recognition and realisation of these two impulses. Rani then suggests that her son should perform the funeral rites of the snake and observe annual ritual in commemoration of him. The annual ritual is an attempt to recall that primal experience of the flaming passion of love and ecstasy, and to draw from it a source of sustenance for life. It is a constant renewal of life energy through deeper contact with the mysteries of life, by getting into that charmed circle – *mandala*.

An interesting and meaningful coincidence occurs, when Rani is struggling with her hair entangled with cobra, and Apanna wakes up hearing Kurudavva's call 'Kapanna' mistaking 'Kapanna' for 'Apanna' and Kurudavva's voice for his mother's. The sense of the merger of Apanna and Kapanna (the two names sound similar too) and his mother and Kurudavva apprehended in the drowsy state and Rani's affinity with Yakhini indicated by her being anointed as a goddess signify that all these represent varying aspects of man-woman relationship ranging from the animalic to the angelic.

Rani refuses to remain trapped in the static image of goddess imposed on her by the patriarchy. Witch and goddess are two important stereotypes, with which patriarchy tries to pigeonhole woman and keep her immobile. Rani comes out of these stereotypes, as illustrated by the play and lives the dynamics of life effortlessly shuttling between various roles of the woman. She becomes a woman of power and self-sacrifice. Her suggestion that her son should lit the funeral pyre of the snake and perform an annual ritual every year for him shows her awareness of the dynamics of life which issue from the mysterious vital forces and operate through the cycle of life. This is represented by the image of *mandala. Mandala* is a complex pattern belonging to Tantra or occultism representing the intricate working of the vital energy. And *Nagamandala*, in that sense, is a highly intricate representation of life forces, a subject has to tap to live a full satisfying life. This also in a way counters the stereotypification of India as a land of mere snakes and monks by the colonial discourse by demonstrating that snakes and monks are not immutable exotic elements but they are marked by complexity and dynamism.

At the end of the play Man wakes up as if from a dream. This is a dream more concrete and more wakeful than reality. This means shaking off of cultural amnesia and waking up to cultural identities. These interconnected fantasies have a strong sense of actuality deeply connected to reality – the reality about the postcolonial interrogation of colonialism or neocolonialism, women's struggle against a patriarchally-controlled society, the vitality and energy of folklore as opposed to dry, dull elitism.

Man undergoes "the death of the author" in order to keep the audience alive and provide space for the reader and to situate the text in an intertextual space. He recognises himself as a site for the criss-cross of several discourses. The intertextual space thus constructed about and through him by the cluster-narratives or folk art and fantasies supported by narration, is an attempt to trace the dramatist's postcolonial subject position in its multiplicity and variability. Here the subject is subjected to the forces of colonialism and elitism and the subject in his role as an agent of change is mainly constructed by nativist cultural discourses. Man here narrates tales as well as listens to them. He listens to the folk voices within him and in his culture. It is fantasy, which recognises the split in the self and which becomes a means of dramatising this split at several levels and in several manners. The author, thus, imagines himself as one among unrecognised folk authors. He aspires for their anonymity to make the text vitally productive and readers/spectators creative participants.

Chandrasekhar Kambar

Chandrasekhar Kambar is another Kannada dramatist, who has been consistently working on folk forms— folk theatres, tales and songs—not only in his plays but also in his poetry and prose. His plays celebrate the primordial as against the local and social mores but they have a strong sense of the place that has certain folk flavour. The idiom he has used in expressing the primordial experiences is from folk cultural expressions. Kambar has stated:

> I belong geographically to a village and sociologically to what was considered to be an oppressed and uneducated class. I am, therefore, a folk person simply because I honestly cannot be anything else. ("Introduction", *Jokumaraswami* XI)

He has come from a blacksmith community, from rustic surrounding that reverberates with rituals and festivities. For him life is a celebration and celebration is for him a primary mode of experience:

> I look around and I look into myself. Both are the parts of the same purpose. What I find is always in terms of plenitude – mad joy, simmering cruelty, pain, dense growth, orgiastic sex, loneliness, and unbelievable gusto of legendary proportion – all of which I celebrate. Celebration is the primary mode of experience for me. ("Introduction" *The Shadow of the Tiger and Other Plays* XII)

He deals mainly with fertility myth and, for that, he turns to folk culture. He looks at folk culture as vital, plentiful and joyous. Rajiv Taranath in his introduction to Kambar's *Jokumaraswami* clarifies:

> And because the celebration has a musicality at once private and shared, the rhythm is at once private and contemporary,

a blend of self and community. ("Introduction", *Jokumaraswami*" IX)

In that sense Kambar is a mythmaker. He uses images and symbols that give dense structure to his play. His *Siri Sampige, Jokumaraswami, The Shadow of the Tiger, Alibaba and the Forty Thieves* and *Tukra's Dreams* are dramatic affirmations of life forces and vital energy.

Siri Sampige

Siri Sampige deals with split personality and the fertility myth based on a folk tale that depicts the relationship between a woman and a cobra, Naga. The same story in different variations has been used as the basis of Girish Karnad's *Nagamandala*. They have used *Yakshagana* style in the presentation of the tale. It involves its distinct form in the use of recitative modes of poetry, melodies of music, rhythm, dance technique and above all costuming and make-up. At the back centre stage sits Bhagavata, the chief director, reciter and conductor of the play (medley) and a *surto* player. At a distance to their right sits the *cende* player.

The play opens with Bhagavata and the chorus singing an invocation to Lord Shiva of Savalangi-Shiva as *Arddhanarishwar*, half-woman-half-man that represents the operative principles of love. This serves the purpose of introducing the theme of split personality indicated by Shiva's *Arddhanarishwar* image, a perfect combination of the body and the mind, the matter and the spirit:

> Before we speak a thousand salutations to you, great Lord Shiva of Savalangi. Split in your divine play into man and wife dancing Nataraja Arddhanariishwar body and mind, spirit and matter you are split into two and beyond duality, hail Shiva! (*Modern Indian Drama*, 335)

It is the divine dance that symbolises the ideal balancing of the body and the mind, the matter and the spirit that humans strive for. It also introduces the theme of snake-human relationship worked out at the vital level. Lord Shiva with King Cobra around his neck and the moon at the crest of his tangled knot of hair represents the interconnection between the netherworld, the earth and the heaven. Here the vital erotic force is linked to reality and spirituality. That perhaps accounts for Naga worship prevalent in the North Karnataka district:

> On the popular level the Naga (snake) worship in the form of *Nagamandala* (a serpentine design) and spirit worship (i.e., to the *Bhutas*) are particular to the region and have great antiquity. Every village in the district has its own *Bhutasthanas*, the origin of which can be traced to pre-historic times. (Vatsayan, 36)

Nagamandalas and *Bhutasthanas* represent the realm of the vital forces and the realm of the spirit longing for the body. They therefore assert the primacy of the body. The play is thus a dramatisation of a significant aspect of Kannada folk life and culture. Naga worship is like Manasa puja in West Bengal, celebrated in Sambhu Mitra's *Chand Banikar Pala,* which has already been discussed.

Mother, one of the important characters in the play addressing the audience, presents the background of the situation. After the death of the king Nagara Nayak of Sivapura, his son Shivanaga is to be coronated. The name Shivanaga suggests combination of Shiva and Naga. But there is an oracle from their family god:

> When his voice breaks he may become a monk,
> When his brother dies he also dies. (335)

When the time for wedding comes Mother persuades him to choose a beautiful princess and marry, but the prince hesitates and postpones his decision. Mother at last chooses Siri Sampige, the daughter of King Pushparaja for him.

When the prince is asleep in his Indranivas palace, he sees in his dream the carved lampstand come to life. Perhaps released from the curse, freed from the stony statuesque existence a beautiful maiden comes to life, leaps with a lamp in her palm and starts dancing:

> The prince is awakened and while he attempts to catch the woman she vanishes dancing inside him. The prince is in a state of high rapture. (342)

She represents his dream-woman he has been longing for. It is his intense imagination that takes a concrete form. He speaks before mother and family elders that they should split his body into equal halves, put the pieces in two pots, bury them among flowers. On the next full-moon day, when they open the two pots, they will see from one pot come out a prince of matchless charm, that is the prince himself. From the other will come out the "palace lamp-maiden", a woman of statue-like beauty holding a lamp in her hand. Then they would get the two married. This is done accordingly. But eventually from one pot comes out a big snake with a precious gem adorning its head, and from another pot emerges the smiling prince. He cannot become *Arddhanarishwar* but becomes Naga and Ishwar (Shiva). The Naga that comes out is the externalisation of his potent masculine energy, the body in its carnal and sexual manifestation that the prince has suppressed in his search for the ideal beauty that is the abstract beauty of the soul.

The prince has to marry Siri Sampige but is not satisfied with her and goes out searching for the lamp-maiden. Every night he goes out to a pond in the forest and keeps looking into the pond. At the touch of his breath, as if angered, the water in the pond trembles, waves rise, break up the reflected clouds and the deep blue sky seems to be sliced by cruel knives. His friend Jawali, who has been following him, reports to the queen:

> His reflection came up there like a floating corpse. The moment he saw it his face shone. Tears of happiness came into his eyes. In his ecstasy no word came from his mouth. As if silently talking with that corpse, he sat there, still. (351)

The prince addresses as maiden to what Jawali describes as the reflection of the prince. He tells Jawali that a maiden comes out of the water. It implies that the maiden is a part of himself, his dream. Here is the counterpointing of two perspectives – one is that of doom, the other is that of dream. It suggests that his pursuit of dream is to lead to his doom. He says:

> Gradually we became, both together an invisible zero, transcending form, becoming the Shivalinga, becoming god."(352)

In his relentless pursuit of spiritual beauty he ignores the physical. On the contrary his wife Siri Sampige seeks the magic of the body, the wonder of physical union, which is provided by Kalinga. Kalinga is the serpent king, the other half of the prince as manifested earlier. This division is like that between Apanna and Naga in *Nagamandala*. The snake stands for the suppressed sexuality, deep inside human body seeking satisfaction. As Bhagavata suggests:

> The serpent has made its dwelling deep inside you. (353)

The union is described through sensuous images, images of fertility and poetically evocative lines:

> Even at this distance the smell of the ploughed earth
> That her body exhales makes me tingle. (354)
> Aha! Her body is like a festival for my aroused
> senses. (355)

Siri Sampige falls under "the wizard's spell" (355). Mother meets Kalinga, who has changed his shape and appears as her son. She is happy to see him. This shows that they are one and same.

I can explain this phenomenon that Siri Sampige with her deep erotic impulse is able to transform her other-worldly husband into a passionate and amorous lover. This is what happens in Karnad's *Nagamandala,* when at night Rani is visited by Naga, who can be the lover-image of her husband, whom she has been able to arouse. Kalinga hints at such a possibility:

> While you were in your bed with your husband, who was lying there like a piece of wood, was there not in the nether region of your mind a king kneeling before you, begging for your love? (357)

Again Kalinga is linked up with the lamp-maiden, when Siri Sampige says:

> Ay! A seven-hooded snake is standing like a lampstand aiming its raised hoods at me. (359)

She seems to be traveling in the world of unconscious. The abstract beauty is transformed into a physical form.

Subsequently Siri Sampige gets pregnant and is suspected by the prince. By denying the body he rejects what the body does but is not aware that the dormant body has been activated and enlivened by Siri Sampige. She is an erotic physical counterpart to the lamp maiden. The prince wants to hold a trial of Sampige. In the assembly of elders it is decided that she will have a snake-ordeal. She lets the snake climb on her body but she is not bitten. She passes the ordeal and is acclaimed as a goddess. A son is born and grows up. The prince keeps guard and finds out that the snake is her lover. Sampige responds to his charge of immorality:

> My immorality started, my lord, when you forgot the body and began craving for the god and slipped away from our bed. In the end you saw a god by taking handfuls of water from the pond. I too took a handful of water and there was a god in my handful too; but if he turned out not to be the same god as yours, is it my fault? I am already half-widow, my lord. You can't understand the grief of one who is always half a widow. When you split yourself you split me also. When you are before me your body is widowed; when I am with him, lying with him, my mind is widowed... A child is born to a widow. (374)

The predicament of Sampige is the predicament of the woman living with a man on his path of renunciation, a man who denounces body as the seat of filth, worms and carnality and opts for the mind, the soul and the spirit. Kalinga happens to be the other side of the prince, the bodily and the sexual revived, regenerated through Sampige's erotic charm and imagination.

The prince is enraged and attacks Kalinga. In the fierce battle Kalinga is killed but in his eyes the prince sees himself and feels his entrails have gone cold. Bhagavata sings:

> In his open eyes the prince saw a wonder unforgettable.
> Looking there – ah ha – himself
> He felt his spine's knot slipping;
> My entrails have gone cold, he said coming to the palace.

He comes back home sick and weak. The prince complains of his navel growing cold, his spine loosening, which is the result of the destruction of the body. He realises:

> When I split myself, we got separated into body and mind. Kalinga became my body. I became the mind. Siri Sampige became pregnant by my body. (377)

He admits before Sampige that she has been misunderstood and asks her to have their son perform the last rites for Kalinga and him. His last words are a plea for integrating the body with the mind:

> Listen, see to it that our son does not split himself. (He dies) (380)

There is a subplot of twins Awali and Jawali, which is a comic parallel to the main plot. They look so much alike that they seem to be the two parts of the same. As the court jesters they provide not only comic relief but also a common sense perspective to the play. Awali and Jawali even start conversation with Bhagavata, complaining of not being properly introduced to the audience thus breaking the dramatic illusion. The riddle they exchange with the woman is another folk form, and the solution gives the identity of the woman as Kamala. In a duel Jawali defeats Awali and is married to Kamala and Awali pitifully leaves for the forest.

The subplot reiterates the thematic development of the main plot. Jawali, who is married to Kamala, thinks all the time of his friend Awali, dreams of his coming back from the forest looking at Kamala and sighing. They are brothers and rivals, mutually bound to each other. They in realistic terms work out what the prince and Kalinga represent at the allegorical level. Kamala is told by the family god that she should first worship a creeper of blooming jasmine on the anthill under the banyan tree, then pluck the flowers, make a garland out of them and put it around her husband's neck, and then he will transform himself into a serpent and unite with her. But Kamala is confused to see the two look-alikes and ultimately takes Jawali with her.

Kamala puts the magic garland around Jawali's neck. Jawali turns into a serpent and indulges in open carnality with her. Awali then thinks of a plan. He boils milk. The smell of the overflowing milk reaches the serpent inside Kamala. The serpent comes out and dips his mouth into the pot and his mouth is burnt and he dies. Blinded by anger and jealousy Awali chops the writhing snake with an axe. Kamala after some days lays eggs. Awali crushes them between his hands. Sad and furious Kamala disappears into the forest. Awali also goes into the forest, looks at the lake water and sees the image of Jawali. He jumps into the water to kill the latter and dies. Kamala's laying is indicative of the consequence of too much carnality. It is the other side of the scale - complete ignorance of the soul. Jawali stands for all sexuality into which he has been transformed by Kamala and Awali for spirituality. They eventually destroy each other.

The entire play is an allegory of the conflict between the body and the soul, the matter and the mind. The traditional value structure that gives the dominant position to the soul and the mind and ignores and suppresses the body is questioned here. Rightly he has used the folk perspective that gives more importance to the culture of the body-dance and the martial art. It is an attempt at reaching out to the state of Shiva – an integration of man, woman and Naga, of male and female principles bound by primordial energy.

The basic difference between Karnad and Kambar in their treatment of the similar folktale is that while the former brings in many other issues like gender the latter concentrates on the aspect of fertility of vitality in society.

JOKUMARASWAMI

Jokumaraswami is Kambar's another important play in which Kambar uses a folk tale of fertility to express his continuing concern with impotence and fertility. Here in this play he has extended its context by including the fertility of land. The folk style used is that of *Bayalata*. *Bayalata* continues the tradition of prologue and epilogue and is full of songs and dances.

The play is an interpretation of a folk myth of Jokumaraswami, a phallic god. He is worshipped even today in the villages of North Karnataka. An annual festival, which normally occurs in August or September on *Jokumar Hunnive* (full-moon night), is named after him. The worship starts on the eighth day (*ashtami*) of the month of *Bhadrapada* (in Oriya it is called *Bhadrava* that falls in the month of September). Women belonging to the castes of fisherman, washerman and line-maker make phallus—shaped idols of Jokumaraswami out of wet clay. Applying butter to the phallus tips they place the idols in a basket. Each idol is packed firmly in an erect position with neem (margosa) leaves. Women carry the baskets on their heads and go from house to house singing songs in praise of Jokumaraswami. Householders give them alms of salt, chillis and tamarind in response to the ritual begging. In some villages the village boys get together and make a large phallus, eight to ten feet long and tip it with lime. At its base they stick hair gathered from a barber-shop. It is believed that women become fertile, if they sit on the phallus. Sometimes snakegourds are placed on baskets. Villagers cook snakegourd as an embodiment of Jokumaraswami and feed it to the husbands of women who are having no issues.

Jokumaraswami is associated with rain. It is believed that even a rainless month will end with a shower on *Jokumar Hunnive.* There are many stories about Jokumaraswami. The common myth behind this goes somewhat like this... Jokumaraswami, the son of Shiva, takes birth on the earth as the son of Ditriadev. From the second day of his birth till the sixth he seduces all the women of the village. On the eleventh the angry cuckolds of the village kill him with ritual cruelty. Wherever his blood falls the earth turns green and fertile. The human fertility is thus related to the fertility of the earth, which is an important aspect of the play.

The plot opens with *Gana Pada* (opening prayer) – the prayer for Lord *Savalangi Shivalinga*—and an appeal to the audience to sit quietly. The invocation of Shiva, the God of fertility, is an appropriate opening for the play, which deals with the theme of fertility. In the prologue that follows Sutradhar asks Himmala to make arrangements for the worship of Jokumarswami, represented in the stage by a snakegourd standing prominently in the middle of a basket filled with vegetables. Usually Ganesh is worshipped in the beginning of a performance. Since the play is about Jokumaraswami and he is the brother of Ganesh there is the justification of his worship. It is sung that if a curry is made out of him and fed to barren women, they will bear children, and if given to husbands they will begin to stick to their homes like aging pet dogs. Mela, who represents the chorus, joins them. No barren woman, as it is expected, comes to take the basket. Shari, the whore at last comes and takes away the sacred basket. This way the prologue sets the framework of the play.

All other scenes are given titles that sum up the contexts of the scenes. This is a Brechtian pattern that the play follows as an alienation effect device. In the scene "Musket God" Kambar packs all the introductory information about the characters and the story, mediated by Sutradhar and Mela. "Musket God" refers to Gowda, the landlord, who is followed by a retinue of four men carrying a musket. With a tinge of satire he is presented as *Dum Dum* God, referring to the sound of explosion of the musket. Another important character is Basanna. Basanna is a young man in the village. Gowda's men have killed his father and his land has been occupied by him on the pretext that he has not repaid his loan. He tells Basanna that his father has been killed by the devil and the field is called devil's field. Gurya, in this scene complains that Gowda's servants have killed his goats. But threatened by Gowda he agrees that his goats have been killed by the devil and Gowda has bought his land. Gowda uses superstition to justify his misdeeds and frighten others into submission. In the village there resides a courageous girl, Ningi, who dares to challenge Gowda. Gowdathi, Gowda's wife, complains that for ten years they have been married but don't have a child. She asks Gowda to come that night and eat the curry of Jokumaraswami. She also asks him to get her a parrot, which indicates her attempt to make her husband surrender to her desire. This scene introduces the themes of exploitation and infertility.

In the scene "Rise and Come, Beloved Parrot" the parrot is described as the harbinger of vitality:

> Bring to the parched earth the season of blossoming
> Flowers, O, bird of distant lands. (17)

The link between human fertility and the fertility of the earth is suggested in the rustic wit of Bassi, Gowdathi's maidservant:

> She smelt like newly ploughed field even at a distance. (18).

She gives a very common sense view of things through suggestive sexual imagery hinting at the impotence of Gowda:

> If the balls don't bless, what can God's blessings do? (19)

In the scene "Bird of the Season", Gowdathi approaches Shari, the whore for Jokumarswami.

The irony is that Gowda is a rich man, a land grabber but impotent, whereas Basanna is poor but virile. Basanna is a rebel, even infuses strength and courage into timid persons. Even Gurya, frightened into cowardly humiliating submission to the point of allowing Gowda to sit on his back, stands up and throws him off, being inspired by Basanna. This scene is entitled as "Paunch Fell down".

After cooking Jokumaraswamy Gowdathi anxiously waits for Gowda to come back so that she will serve him food but is informed by his servants that he has gone to sleep in "the devil's field" to vindicate his ownership of the field accepting the challenge of Basanna. Disappointed Gowdathi sings of her bird to return to her nest.

When in the night Gowda's servants are guarding "the devil's field", Basanna suddenly attacks them, snatches away their guns and chases them away. He comes to know from them that Gowda is in Shari's house. He then goes to sleep in the cottage. The Gowdathi then comes with Jokumaraswami curry looking for Gowda and runs into Basanna with Gowda's blanket on him, and offers him the curry. He eats the curry and tells her that her husband is impotent, cannot even get her a parrot and after he has eaten Jokumaraswami he has become her lover. He can give her full sexual pleasure and make her a mother. The scene is rightly titled as "The Bird Is Caught". Basanna and Gowdathi go on romancing. He gives her a parrot. The parrot is a symbol of multiple significance. It stands for the lover, the child. In a rustic sense it can be interpreted as phallus too.

"The Defeat of Dum Dum God" depicts how Ningi and her lover Gurya together face Gowda and defeat him. Gurya says, "Gowda, Basanna had a parrot and he gave it to Gowdathi. Gowdathi swallowed it, and now her tummy is like this!"(41) After marrying Ningi Gurya gathers courage enough to challenge Gowda.

The last scene, "The God Is Slain", presents the killing of Basanna, who emerges as an incarnation of the fertility god Jokumaraswami. Basanna has been known for his sexual exploits in the village like the young god. When he is attacked by Gowda's men in the night he asks Gowdathi, "Run and save the parrot's life"(43). Here the parrot implies the real parrot and the baby in her womb. His death signals the beginning of a new era, inspires people to rise against tyranny, to claim their own rights to the land they till and make productive the land, that the landlord has turned unproductive through sheer negligence and inattention.

The playwright combines the socio-political issue of the right to ownership of land with the issue of potency and productivity. That he who tills the land should own the land is taken literally and symbolically. Jokumaraswamy worship stands for activating the connexions with the sources of the vital forces or primordial energies, that gives people both potency and rebellious spirit. Potency and rebellious spirit, virility and courageousness are joined together. Full of songs and dances it is a ritual theatre: one play that can be compared with *Jokumaraswamy* is Mahasweta Devi's *Aajir*, which deals with the same theme of the ownership of the land and fertility. Aajir, the bonded labourer, while fighting for his freedom from the slavery of several generations finds himself being wooed by the wife of the impotent landlord. While in the former the theme of fertility is emphasised, in the latter the socio-economic issues are foregrounded.

The Shadow of the Tiger

The Shadow of the Tiger is another play that interprets a folktale seeking to probe the complex relation between truth and lies, reality and illusion. A demon appears in the shape of a tiger in a village. Gowda goes out to kill it but is instead killed by the tiger, who in the disguise of Gowda, enters the latter's house, lives as

Gowda in his house. Gowdathi, Gowda's wife, gets pregnant, becomes half-mad, and impregnated with the tiger's spirit asks her son to bring the tiger's milk. Ramgoda, her son goes in search of the tiger's milk into the forest and finds out that his father has been transformed into a tiger and the tiger has taken the place of his father. He returns and finds out that his mother bears the seeds of her demon husband. But he cannot take revenge. He faces a Hamletian dilemma. The search for one's real parents becomes a metaphor for the search for the origin and identity of man. Man is a blending of human and demon. It is difficult to disentangle one from the other.

Chandrasekhar Kambar's uniqueness lies in his consistent exploration of folk culture in his drama. Almost all his plays deal with the theme of fertility, and for this he chooses the folk myth of fertility. He has observed that the socio-psychological imbalance is caused by lack of sexual pleasure and productivity in man and woman. His plays, therefore, are the celebrations of the vital forces of life, the ritual of primordial energy. The neglect of the body for spiritual life, as in the case of the Prince in *Siri Sampige* or for materialistic greed as in the case of Gowda in *Jokumaraswami* results in the erosion of what can be called *elan vital* that leads to sterility. What Kamber suggests is the need for the renewal and activating of man's connection with the source of the vitality through the exercise of body and mind, physical and mental faculties, instinct, imagination and intuition. These activities and exercises are amply provided by our folk culture.

Malayalam Drama

K.N. Panikkar

Kevalam Narayan Panikkar opposes the present practice of intercultural rejuvenation of home cultures by acts of productive reception of foreign cultures. His theatre does so not by refusal or direct opposition but by theatrical acts of intracultural rejuvenation, without injects of the foreign culture as a serum. The rationalist view of the world urged upon Asians entails a fundamental criticism of indigenous culture. It denounces it as non-rational (magical, superstitious, religious). But this cannot explain the reason for the survival of ritual practices even in an urbanised world. Intracultural practice by giving currency to inherited culture has certaiin political significance in this context. It is to foster a community spirit, shared living, social solidarity in the society threatened by disintegrating forces. Kevalam Narayan Panikkar is a leading exponent of this theatre practice. He is the writer and director of the Sapnam Institute of Performing Arts in Trivandrum, and has been active in this field

The Lone Tusker

Panikkar has used Kuttiyattam performance in his *The Lone Tusker*. Kuttiyattam, according to Vatsayan, is the only surviving tradition of Sanskrit theatre in Kerala but it has unmistaken links with and elements from the folk tradition. The narrator of the theatre is called Chakyar, who belongs to a community of artistes who perform the Kootha and Koottiyattam in the Koothampalam (the space for staging Kootha). The Chakyars belong to the Ambalavasi (temple dwellers) caste, an intermediate group between the Brahmins and the Nairs. There has been a practice in Kerala that any son other than the eldest in a Nambudri family can marry in a Nair family, and out of this Chakyar community is formed.

Vatsayan has explained the relevance of Kuttiyattam in the present time:

> However the secret of the survival of the Kuttiyattam lies as much in the ability of the Chakyar community to safeguard and preserve tradition of an earlier epoch as in their ability to adapt to new situations, to respond to local and immediate concerns, and to be flexible enough to be able to give their presentation contemporary validity and significance. (*The Traditional Indian Theatre*, 21)

This flexibility makes it convenient for Panikkar to use this form.

Chakyar moves from place to place carrying a knapsack showing performances. He is the lone adventurer in carrying on this traditional theatre, when it is being looked down upon by elitists, and in using it for modern situation, when traditionalists are up against any attempt to dilute it. Chakyar in the beginning asserts:

> It is a purely Lokadharmi play, by this I simply mean that the story really took place. It is a tale of worldly affairs. I will certainly do my best to make it a Natyadharmi play; in other words, I shall try to add necessary embellishments..(*Modern Indian Drama* 325)

On the way, as Chakyar narrates, he finds a lone tusker, who has left the rut and broken away from the herd. He decides, "Come what may, let me try a bit of acting in front of the elephant. If I am blessed enough the elephant may be frightened by my performance and go back" (326). But slowly he identifies himself with the lone tusker. His transformation is from an actor to a performer and then to a character, from a human to an animal. He is caught by a woodsman and treated as an animal. He is taken to Mooppanar, the headman. Chakyar is an artiste, who treads a lonely path but his performance brings collective feeling. Mooppanar forces him to open his knapsack. In it there are two or three withered garlands, some bracelets and a headdress and a pair of *Kuzithala* or cymbals. He explains that his beloved Nagiyar used to keep rhythm with *Kuzithala*. She made a mistake in the rhythm during the performance. So he quarrelled with her and came away. This shows that the theatre is his life.

The woodsman plays on *Kuzithala* and dances. This makes the beginning of their initiation into the performance. They first want to offer Chakyar as a sacrifice to Kali, which is another ritual they believe in. They ask him to do drama. Chakyar offers to build a house for them. He enacts the building of the house amidst drumbeats. In course of the enactment he asks them to join him. They work together as in the background the drumbeats become faster. "Now the woodsmen seem to be carried away by the illusion.... They join hands with the Chakyar in lifting the log and start behaving as if they are bearing the entire weight" (331). Chakyar describes them as "wild cats lifting the beam", or "two lizards perched on the ceiling" suggesting that that they are bearing the wood may be a reality or illusion. Whatever it may be this act expresses the community spirit, which folk culture fosters. It is through his performance that he escapes death. The play ends with an epilogue, a song of benediction:

Who has won and who has lost
I am not eager to learn
To wish all happiness to you
Bharatavakya will be sung. (332)

Chakyar plays the role of an elephant carrying the log. He is the carrier of the tradition that is useful for our life as the log is.

This vignette is a celebration of community spirit that has been threatened by disintegrating forces. Kuttiyattam is performed in open space, actors move in and out of the spectators breaking down the boundaries between the stage and the audience. Thus the notion of the community spirit, shared living, social solidarity is extended to include the world at large.

THE RIGHT TO RULE

In *The Right to Rule (Koyama)* Panikkar has used many folk forms—Kuttiyattam, Teyyam and Kathakali. Full of music and dance characters, images and language build up the theme of the fight between good and evil. Sutradhar introduces the theme:

I bring you today a tale of wonder
A tale of passion, of burning love,
A tale that's not a tale but true.
(*The Right to Rule and The Domain of the Sun,* 10)

He is soon surrounded by three masked men representing the Present, the Past and the Future in an attempt to kill him so that the performance can be liberated from the rule and discipline imposed by the Sutradhar, who is from the Sanskrit tradition. They take 'the stage manager' for the 'the stage-manipulator' and for 'the master-manipulator of state affairs'. The art and life are linked up here. These masked characters appear as Kathakali actors, who actually evolved form from the folk tradition and represents the spirit of freedom. The opposition between the classical and the folk is here hinted at.

Sundari in the play is the archetypal lover. For her "love is nature's eternal pilgrimage in search of the skies" (13). Paimkurali, the temple cow is the eternal mother, Kamadhenu. Nayadi is the archetypal hunter, who stands for the primordial forces of life. He gives the king the bow and the arrow and teaches him the art of using them. Kshetrapalan is "the master manipulator of state affairs" referred to earlier in the play. He begs of Nayadi the bow and the arrow and gets them. In the guise of the king he approaches Sundari and deceives her into loving him. Paimkurali recoils in shock and rage at this and expresses her anguish:

> Evil has erupted and submerged the good.
> The reed that was planted
> To bear fruit
> Has borne venom instead.

The king has become a tyrant surrounded by sycophants, taken over by royal splendour and grandeur. Masked men present the vision of bestiality and destruction, the impending Kaliyuga. Nayadi declares, "Thus ends a generation"(29).

The king is to perform the rite of Hiranyagarbha, that is, he is to enter through the mouth of the sacred cow and come out through the tail to purify himself. Vidushaka (Jester) and other attendants reverse the process by entering through the tail coming out of the mouth. The result is they "emerge wearing monstrous expressions"(31). They become more impure by defiling the mother principle. They, including the king, intone the parody of mantras. Even though the king has observed the ritual properly he cannot be pure, because it is the purity of heart that matters, not the outward ritual alone.

Sundari comes to know Kshetrapalan has deceived her. She writes a note and asks him to give it to the king. He takes the note but later on tears it into shreds. Masked men capture him and drive him away. The evil spirit possesses the king. Nayadi then appears as an exorcist and starts exorcising the king by chanting mantras. They infuse the primordial forces into him. Masked men tell the king Sundari's love for him:

> She is always around you, mingled with the soil
> Wherever within the green depths of the earth's
> Birth chamber..(37)

Sundari stands for the Prakriti, the female principle to be united with the Purush, the male principle, that the king is to embody.

But evil forces disrupt the process of union. She is finally united with the king.

At the end Sundari opens her bundle and "takes out, one by one, the mask of a cow and the limbs of her child. She looks at each object aghast" (39). This shows that her struggle against the evil is not over. Her child from fake Kshetrapalan has to be sacrificed for her new life with the king. She is to take the place of the sacred cow. She is to attain that state of eternal motherhood. She is the spiritual progeny of Paimkurali. This struggle for perfection continues. There are sufferings, agonies and heartbreak in the way. There is no finality. Masked men who represent Time, the eternal flow of time sing:

> Behold
> The incompleteness that writhes
> At the edge of the sweeping sword!
> To these sobs of unending agony, hark.
> The eternal deliverance that man must attain
> To see the rays of tomorrow's dawn,
> How much longer is the road?
> How much more must we travel. (39)

The play ends with a note of hope with the image of the masked men, leading the actors "with their sticks raised in posture of hope" (39). The play suggests that he who fights against the evil, has the right to rule.

The Right to Rule is just a piece of poetry charged with passion and fervour, highly ritualistic and intensely moving. With vigorous music, dance, acting and declamatory style skillfully used it overwhelms the audience with a sense of mystery as Artaud's Theatre of Cruelty does. The comparison is not exactly intercultural which Panikkar opposes, for it is to be noted that Artaud himself was influenced by Eastern theatre, particularly by Bali's theatre. Panikkar's is a theatre of ritual, a kind of liturgy that really releases tremendous life force with which it overwhelms the audience and draws them into the mysteries of life.

TEYYATEYYAM

Panikkar's recent play *Teyyateyyam* (Once a good dancer, Now a godhead) takes the North Kerala folk tradition of *Teyyam*. By learning it and practising it in a new modern context, he uses it as an allegory of modern life. *Teyyam* is a Dravidian ritual, the aim being ultimately to combine the elements of ritual with the dramatic. In the *Padayani* ritual of central Kerala village men don the masks of gods and come in a procession accompanied by flaming torches, singing and *Padayani* songs. The emphasis is more on the accomplishment of the ritual than on the completion of the performance.

Teyyam means the deification of the spiritual and the word '*Teyyam*' derives from Deivam or God. Every human being, it is believed, is transformed into *Teyyam* after death. The social rationale behind this is that persons who suffer untimely deaths or who suffer injustice in an unequal society (as well as those, whose earthly life needs to be rewarded) achieve deification. *Teyyam* deities were propitiated for the welfare of the community, village or individual through dance, drama, music and poetry. They in turn appear before the devotees through the medium who may be a priest, a chosen person and grant them their wishes.

The second type of *Teyyam* is of gods whose different reincarnations are enacted as *Teyyam*. These gods are Dravidian, the protectors of humanity from natural disasters. Even demon gods such as Ravana are included in the list. The reason is that there is no distinction between hero and demon gods.

In *Teyyateyyam* there are two parallel plots which eventually merge. In the first it is the harvest time, and Ramunni, an agricultural worker and *Teyyam* dancer, hears of the attempted seduction and rape of his girl friend Kannipoo by the local landlord Mekkanthala. Ramunni, after killing Mekkanthala, elopes with Kannipoo. Kannipoo's father Salguni is outraged by the incident and immediately wants retaliation for the unlawful abduction of his daughter. Ramunni's mother appears and informs that her son is undergoing a forty-one day penance in preparation for the *Teyyam*, for which, she assures, he will return to the village to dance. The villagers kill Ramunni at the end.

Running parallel to the plot is the villagers' version of the *Ramayana*, in which the villain Ravana arrives on shore to continue his plundering of wealth because he believes all things good on the earth should belong to him. In this version Sita becomes

Poonkanni (played by the same performer as Kannipoo in the first plot). Poonkanni is abducted by Paranki (the villagers' name for Ravana) and taken to his ship. The same actor, who plays Ramunni, plays Paranki. Beppooran (the monkey-god Hanuman, and friend of Rama in the *Ramayana*) sets off in search of Poonkanni. Coming to know that Paranki's strength lies in the magic belt tied around the waist, Beppooran steals his belt, and is thus able to beat him to death. Subsequently Paranki is deified in keeping with Teyyam tradition that deification is not based on moral judgement. As this character Paranki is played by Ramunni, who has returned to the play, the two story lines merge. The villagers armed with sticks approach Ramunni playing Paranki and the personalities of both characters are confused. So the characters from the second plot (Paranki) and also from the first plot (Ramunni) are beaten to death. Consequently there is the *Teyyam* of a *Teyyam*, hence the title *Teyyateyyam*.

The irony in the play is that Ramunni is killed for avenging an act of injustice, an attempted rape and he then appears to be an innocent victim. But at the same time Ramunni has abducted rather than eloped with another man's daughter. Both Ramunni and Paranki are ultimately deified.

The villager first transforms by acts of penance into the performer, and then from the performer by learning the dance tradition into the character. Ramunni, the performer, next transforms into Paranki *Chamundi* (the deified Paranki) and still further into character – the deification of Ramunni. Brian Singleton has commented, "...and so the author, Panikkar, takes the mirroring of the two roles and reflects them into infinity. The essence of this modern theatre is the dramatisation of the impossibility of totally separating performer from the role" (*Indian Literature* XLV No. 5, pg. 205). The play ends with the justification of *Teyyam* tradition:

> Thus, man enjoys creating the tradition of *Teyyams*
> Man, human being, a combination of good and evil.
> Even when a Teyyam is created for an evil reason
> Let us praise good deeds
> And finish this dance performance.
>
> (*Indian Literature* XLV No. 5, pg. 165)

The drama does not unfold chronologically. The villagers' story and the *Ramayana* story are woven together textually, achieved in performance through the use of chorus. They all both antagonists and protagonists emerge from and return to the chorus. Character identities are transient and fleeting, for as the narrative moves on, the performers must move from one plot to the next and also take part in the chorus. Costumes are minimal. All action is stylised. There is no pretence for realism.

The play also denies any boundary between the spectator and the performer. Although spectators are not invited to perform, the performance of *Teyyateyyam* can take place in an open space with the performers on the same level as the audience. The actors can emerge from anywhere. It does much also to suggest that theatre take place in life. Resistance therefore becomes theatrical as well as social, religious and non-rational.

6

Folk Forms as Dramatic Strategy in the Post-Independence Indian Drama

I have discussed thirty-two plays of twenty-five playwrights covering eight major Indian languages: Hindi, Marathi, Bengali, Oriya, Assamese, Manipuri, Kannada and Malayalam. In course of my study, as I have already stated, I faced certain constraints such as my lack of knowledge or lack of adequate knowledge in various regional languages, the non-availability of many texts, in original or in translation, of critical materials and the limited scope in seeing the performances, folk or modern. Though the discussion, as the title suggests, is limited to a particular period and a particular dramatic aspect, there are many other relevent elements, which have been brought in. It is a comparative, interdisciplinary, cross-cultural study, which seeks to combine folklore, literary and performance studies.

The use of the elements of folk culture by the post-independence Indian playwrights is a part of the nativist project of making use of the indigenous knowledge system in meeting the present problems that afflict us. This is in response to the constant denigration of folk culture as irrational, superstitious and religious under the elitist Western gaze. This can be related to a larger theoretical perspective. Derrida's repudiation of logocentrism, denial of the centre, emphasis on free play of signs and signifying systems has, in fact, freed human discourses from the hegemonic control. His refutation of Eurocentrism paves the way for many alternatives and so the recognition of Blacks, Native

Americans, the Third World and Women as distinct and distinguishable categories. His challenge to the autonomy of rationalism leads to the acceptance of the non-rational as a part of life. Belief in magic, miracle, rituals, cult worship that has moved the life of the people for ages provides many alternative approaches to life. Foucoult's emphasis on the local gives credence to the folk culture, which can be described as the universalisation of "the local". The post-modernist's rejection of the grand narrative explains the rejection of the elitist, the Western and consequently the revival of folk culture.

The imperialist design of the Western representation of the East as a strategy to internationalise colonial values, to make the people of the East look down upon their own values, tradition, knowledge system and modes of being and doing has been exposed by Gandhi's *Hindswaraj*, Franz Fannon's *Wretched of the Earth* and *Black Skin and White Mask*, Edward Said's *Orientalism* and Gauri Viswanathan's *Masks of Conquest*. The West also constructed the East through exoticisation, and Eastern subjects often absorbed this fantasy into their own self-perception. Homi K. Bhabha, through his concepts like "ambivalence" and "mimicry", pointed to the fact that the colonised through imitation ridicules the coloniser. But this, ridicule, we find, is a byproduct of imitation. According to Althurser coloniser forms the colonised subject through the repressive state apparatus like police, army, legislature, and ideological state apparatus like language, school, church in the process of colonisation. Gayatri Spivak points out that the subaltern cannot speak. All these theoreticians have not talked about resistance. In Aijaz Ahmad's words, "Western representations have been in various ways received, accepted, modified, challenged, overthrown or reproduced by the intelligentsia of the colonial countries, which these theoreticians have not talked about" (*In Theory*, p. 172).

Assimilation and subversion are the two general strategies used by our post-independence dramatists. They assimilate the relevant elements of the folk and the classical and the Western cultures and also try to subvert the elitist and Western hegemony. They address the opposition between the West and the non-West, as well as the oppositions within the anti-colonial discourse in terms of class, caste and gender, opposition between the elite and the folk, between totalitarian nationalism and local and attempt to dismantle the hierarchy between these oppositions specificities.

The entire thrust of the use of folk elements in post-independence Indian drama is that it gives a common man's perspective to the issues that the dramatists address. Tanvir's *Charandas Chor* presents a plebian point of view. So also the plays of Karnad, Kambar, Pannikar, Mahasweta Devi, Bibhas Chakraborty, Manoranjan Das.

Critiquing the contemporary situation is another purpose of this strategy. There are a lot of subversive elements in the folk forms that are deployed to question the prevailing social inequality, gender discrimination, regional imbalance, exploitation and corruption in public life. Mahasweta Devi's *Aajir*, Karnad's *Hayavadana* and Kambar's *Jokumaraswami* are the severe indictment of social inequality. Saonli Mitra's *Nathabati Anathabati* and *Katha Amruta Samana* present the plight of woman in a patriarchal society. Surendra Varma's *From Sunset to Sunrise*, Karnad's *Nagamandala*, Bibhas Chakraborty's *Madhab Malanchhi Kaheniya*, Manoranjan Das's *Nandika Keshari* are some of the plays, which give central role to women. Exploitation is the theme of a number of plays like Utpal Dutt's *Surya Shikaar*, Devi's *Aajir*, Tendulkar's *Ghashiram Katwal*, Arun Sarma's *Buranjipat*, Satish Bhattacharya's *Maharaja*, Ramesh Panigrahi's *Mahanatak*, Karttik Rath's *Bahniman*, Bijay Satpathy's *Ei Je Surjya Uen*, etc. Tanvir's *Charandas Chor*, Bajahat's *Birgati*, deal with corruption in society. Karnad's *Hayavadana* and Kanhailal's *Pebet* are implicitly and explicitly concerned with regional imbalance. The theme of fertility is mainly the theme of Kambar's plays. All these themes in combination with each other are often found in many such plays. For example, Kambar in his plays deals with the themes of fertility and exploitation. Class, caste differences and gender discrimination go together in many plays like *Hayavadana*, *Nagamandala*, *Aajir*, *Nandika Keshari* and so on. Tendulkar's *Ghashiram Katwal*, Asgar Bajahat's *Birgati* are reflections on the political intrigues and manipulation going on in our society. *Birgati* and Harichandan's *Kaluribenta* show how corrupt bureaucrats manipulate and control the system resulting in the harassment of honest and common people.

There are various methods of using the folk elements. Playwrights sometime interpret certain existing folk tales as reflections on our present day situation. Tanvir's *Charandas Chor* interprets a Rajasthani folk tale, Karnad's *Hayavadana,* a Sanskrit folktale from Somadev's *Kathasaritasagar* and *Nagamandala,* a Kannada folktale. The plays of Chandrasekhar Kambar are rewritings of existing Kannada folktales. He has even taken a folktale from *Arabian Nights* for his *Alibaba and Forty Thieves.* Sambhu Mitra's *Chand Banikar Pala,* Bibhas Chakraborty's *Madhab Malanchhi Kaheniya,* Kanhailal's *Pebet* are such other examples.

In some cases playwrights create the folktales of their own with folktale characters, atmosphere and motifs. Surendra Varma's *From Sunset to Sunrise,* Asgar Bajahat's *Birgati,* Badal Sircar's dramatisation of Premendra Mitra's fairy tales, Ramesh Panigrahi's *Mahanatak,* Bijay Satpathy's *Ei Je Surjya Uen,* Arun Sarma's *Buranjipat,* Satish Bhattacharya's *Maharaja* come under this category.

Utpal Dutt's *Hunting the Sun* (Surya *Shikaar*), Manoranjan Das' *Nandika Keshari* attempt to blend history, legend, myth and folk forms. Panikkar's *Teyyateyyam* combines the folk form of Teyyam, the myth of *Ramayana,* and reality. Ratan Thiyam's *Chukravuyha* is a unique example of the blending of myth and Manipuri folk form. Mahasweta Devi's *Aajir* implicitly alludes to the myth of Harishchandra and Rama and the ritual of the prostitute walking naked in the new moon night unnoticed by people to bring water from the king's lake as a way of propitiating Lord Indra to send rain to the earth.

A folk narrative can be even used as a structural pattern in a play. An Oriya folk narrative of an innocent crow being deceived forms the structural pattern of Niladri Harishchandan's *Kaluribenta.* Folk forms like *Yakshagana* (Kannada), *desianata* (Oriya), *yatra, pala,* (Bengali, Oriya), *nautanki* (Hindi), Manipuri martial art, etc are used as structural patterns for many plays.

Apart from the fact that the content of the plays is derived from folk culture the style of presentation in many cases are folk style. Saonli Mitra uses Bengali *pala* and Chhatisgarhi Pandavani to present the story of Draupadi in *Nathabati Anathabat* and stories of Satyabati, Gandhari, Kunti and Draupadi in *Katha Amruta Samana.* The forms of presentation of *Ghashiram Kotwal* are those of *Lavani, Dasavatar* and *Gondhal*. Karnad and Kambar use *Yakshagana* style. Manoranjan Das adopts *Desianata* style for *Nandika Keshari*. Often many folk forms are selectively and relevantly combined to give the entire play an identity of a folk theatre.

Whatever may be the forms, strategies and purposes of the use of folk elements in the post-independence Indian drama the entire exercise is to build up an indigenous theatre mode, an 'authentic' Indian theatre. The word 'authentic' is used in a relative sense, for there can be nothing called pure and authentic as every mode of being and living is a mixture of several elements drawn from several sources. The term is used here to describe typically Indian situation, its local flavour and traditions. This does not mean total rejection of Western elements, it is rather selective appropriation of them to serve the Indian theatre. Indian elements and for that purpose Indian folk elements are foregrounded in such plays.

There is a network of connections that hold the plays in Indian languages together. For instance, if Telugu, Tamil, Kannada and Malayalam are connected to one another at one level Telugu is related to Oriya at another level and so on. There is common concern in terms of class, caste, and gender within and across linguistic boundaries. The concepts such as Pirandello's metatheatrical structure, Brecht's alienation effect, Artaud's theatre of cruelty, Jerzy Grotowsky's Poor theatre, Joshep Chaikin's Open Theatre are located in and related to our folk theatre modes.

What is most important is that the folk forms should be deployed as a part of overall dramatic design so far as they help in the representation of reality, and our present-day situation. The folk traditions can also be modified, blended with other elements, classical or Western to form a new dramatic strategy. The folk forms for the sake of folk forms will rather lead to a kind of fundamentalism. The dramatists should make relevant and selective use of folk elements to represent their own sense of reality. It should not turn into a fashion, there should not be any attempt to exoticise our folk life and make it a marketable commodity for foreign elitist views.

What I emphasise in this work is the vital plurality of India, the differences that are very productive and fascinating. Its diverse folk traditions and its theatrical activities best represent this mosaic of Indian culture across the country. The various ways of the manipulation of multiple folk forms in various Indian language plays in different regions after independence for different purposes, as discussed, represent this multicultural, multilingual mosaic.

Bibliography

Ahmad, Aijaz. *In Theory: Classes, Nations, Literatures*. New Delhi: Oxford U.P., 1992.

Alekar, Satish. *The Dread Departure (Mahanirvan)*, Trans from Marathi, Gauri Deshpande, Culcutta: Seagull Bokks, 1989.

Anantha Murthy, U.R. "On Being a Writer in India" *Tender Ironies: A Tribute to Lothar Lutze*. Eds. Dilip Chitre et. al. Delhi: Manohar, 1994.

Anderson, Benedict. *Imagined Communities: Reflections on the Origin and Spread of Nationalism*. New York: Verso, 1990.

Alhusser, Louis. "Ideology and Ideological State Apparatus" from Ben Brewster. *Lenin & Philosophy, and other Essays*: 127-88. New York: Monthly Review Press, 1921.

Artaud, Antonin. *The Theatre and Its Double* Trans. Mary Caronine Richards. New York: Grove, 1958.

Ascroft, Bill, Gareth Griffiths and Helen Tiffin. *The Empire Writes Back*. London: Methuen.

Awasthi, Suresh. "Theatre of Roots: Encounter with Tradition". *TDR* 33 4 (1989): 48-69.

Bajahat, Asgar. *Birgati* (Hindi). Delhi: Prachi Prakashan, 1995.

Bakhtin, Mikhail. *Problems of Dostoevsky's Poetics*, Ed. & Trans. Caryl Emerson. Manchester: Manchester University Press, 1984.

_______________. Rabelais and His World Trans. Helen Iswolsky, Bloomington: Indiana University Press, 1984.

Barthes, Roland. "The Death of the Author". *Modern Criticism and Theory: A Reader*. Ed. David Lodge. New York: Longman Inc. Ltd. 1998.

Bhabha, Homi K. *The Location of Culture*. New York: Routledge, 1994.

Bharati, Dharmavir. *Andhayuga* (Hindi). Allahabad: Kitab Mahal, 2000.

Bharucha, Rustom. *The Theatre of Kanhailal: Pebet and Memoirs of Africa* (The Translation from the Performance Text in Manipuri with Introduction). Calcutta: Seagull Books, 1992.

Bhattacharya, Satish. *Maharaja* (Assamese). Guwahati: Rajendra Mohan Sarma. Chandia Prakash, 3 Ed. 2002.

Chakrabarty, Bibhas. *Madhab Malanchhi Kaheniya* (Bengali). Calcutta: Srusti Prakashan, 2002.

Chatterjee, Partha. *Nationalist and the colonial World.* Minnesota: University of Minnesota Press, 1986.

Clark, Katerina and Michael Holquist. *Mikhail Bakhtin: The Dialogical Principle.* Cambridge : Havard University Press, 1984.

Das, Manoranjan. *Nandika Keshari* (Oriya). Cuttack : Nalanda, 1992.

Das, Sisir. *Bagh* (Bengali). Calcutta: Papyrus, 1996.

_______________ . "Construction of Indian Literature". *New Comparison* (23), 1997.

_______________ . *A History of Indian Literature 1810–1910.* Delhi: Sahitya Akademi, 1991

_______________ . *A History of Indian Literature 1911–1956.* Delhi: Sahitya Akademi, 1995.

_______________ . "The Idea of an Indian Literature". *The Idea of an Indian Literature: A Book of Readings.* Ed. Sujit Mukherjee. Mysore: Central Institute of Indian Languages, 1981.

Das, Yugal. *Bayanar Khol* (Assamese). Barpeta: Bangabadi Prakashani, 4th Ed. 2002.

Deshpande, G.P. Ed. *Modern Indian Drama: An Anthology.* New Delhi: Sahitya Akademi, 2000.

Devi, Mahasweta. "Aajir". *Mahasweta Devi's Five Plays.* Trans. From Original Bengali and Introduction by Samik Bandyopadhyay. Calcutta: Seagull Books, 1986.

Devy, G.N. *After Amnesia: Tradition and Change in Indian Literary Criticism.* Bombay: Orient Longman, 1992.

Dodiya, Jaydipsinh. Ed. *The Plays of Girish Karnada: Critical Perspectives.* New Delhi: Prestige, 1999.

Dutt, Utpal. "Hunting the Sun" Trans. From Bengali by the author. *Modern Indian Drama.* Ed. Deshpande.

Eschmann, Annecharlott, Henman Kulke, Gaya Charan Tripathy. Eds. *The Cult of Jagannath and the Regional Tradition of Orissa.* New Delhi: Manohar Publications, 1978.

Foucault, Michel. *Discipline and Punish,* Trans. Alan Sheridal, New York: Vintage Books, 1979.

______________ . *History of Sexuality*, Trans. Robert Hurky, New York: Vintage Books, 1985.

George, K.M. *Modern Indian Literature: An Anthology Vol. 1.* Delhi: Sahitya Akademi, 1992.

Greenblatt, Stephen, "Culture", Critical Terms for Literary Study, Eds. Lentricchia, Frank of Thomas McLaughlin, Chicago: University of Chicago Press, 1990.

Harichandan, Niladri Bhushan. "Kaluribenta". *Jatayura Chhinna Dena* (Oriya). Cuttack: Arya Prakashan, 1998.

Irigaray, Luce. *This Sex Which Is Not One*. Trans. Catharine Porter & Carolyn Burke. Ithaca: Cornell University Press, 1985.

Jackson, Rosemary. *Fantasy: The Literature of Subversion*. London: Metheun & Co. Ltd. 1981.

Kambar, Chandrasekhar. *Siri Sampige*. Trans. From Kannada by Bowena Hill with K.P. Vasudevan and N.S. Ramaswamy. *Modern Indian Drama*. Ed. Deshpande.

______________ . *Jokumaraswamy*, Trans. From Kannada. Rajiv Taranath. Calcutta: Seagull Books 1989.

Kamble, N.D. *Bonded Labour in India*. New Delhi: Uppal, 1982.

Karnad, Girish. *Hayavadana*. Trans. from Kannada, The Author. *Modern Indian Drama*. Ed. G.P. Deshpande. New Delhi: Sahitya Akademi, 2000.

______________ . "Introduction to Three Plays: *Nagamandala, Hayavadana, Tughlaq* ". *The Plays of Girish Karnad*. Ed. Jaydipsinh Dodiya, 1999.

______________ . *Nagamandala*. Trans. Author. Bombay: Oxford University Press, 1990.

Lyotard, Jean Francois *The Postmodern Condition: A Report of Knowledge.* Minneapolis: University, Minnesota Press, 1984.

Mahadevan, Anand. "Switching Heads and Cultures: Transformation of an Indian Myth by Thomas Mann and Girish Karnad". *Comparative Literature*. Winter 2002, Vol. 54, No. 1. 23-41.

Malick, Javed. "Introduction". Tanvir. *Charandas Chor*. Calcutta: Seagull Books, 1996.

Mee, Erin B. "Hayavadana: Model of Complexity. *Girish Karnad's Plays: Performance and critical Perspectives*. Ed. Tutun Mukherjee, New DElhi: Peneraft International, 2006.

Mitra, Sambhu. *Chand Banikar Pala* (Bengali). Calcutta : S.C. Sircar & Sons. Pvt. Ltd. 7th Ed. 2002.

Mitra, Saonli. *Nathabati Anathabati* (Bengali). Calcutta: Amit Sircar, 1983 *Katha Amruta Saman* (Bengali). Calcutta: Amit Sircar, 1990.

Montrose, Louis A. "Professing the Renaissance: The Poetics and Politics of Culture". *The New Historicism*. Ed. H. Aram Veeser. New York: Routledge, 1989.

Mukherjee, Sujeet. "Towards a Literary History of India". *The Idea of an Indian Literature: A Book of Readings*. Ed. Sujeet Mukherjee. Mysore: Central Institute of Indian Languages, 1981.

Mukherjee, Tutun Ed. *Girish Karnad's Plays. Performance and Critical Perspectives*. Delhi: Pencraft International, 2006.

Narasimhaih, C.D. *The Function of Criticism in India: Essays in Indian Response to Literature*. Mysore: Central Institute of Indian Languages, 1986.

Nemade, Bhalchandra: "Nativism in Literature". Trans. From Marathi by Arvind Dixit and edited by Makarand Paranjape. *Nativism: Essays in Criticism*. Ed. Paranjape. New Delhi: Sahitya Akademi. 1997.

Panigrahi, Ramesh Prasad. *Mahanatak* (Oriya). Cuttack: Orissa Book Store, 1981.

Panikkar, K.N. "The Lone Tusker (Ottayam)". Trans. From Malayalam, K.S. Narayan Pillai. *Modern Indian Drama*. Ed. Deshpande.

________________ . *The Right to Rule (Koyma) and The Domain of the Sun (Suryasthana)*. Trans. from Malayalam by Paul Mathew and by R. Gopalakrishnan. Calcutta: Seagull Books 1989.

________________ . "Teyyateyyam". *Indian Literature* (205) 146 – 165.

Panja, Sarmistha. Ed. *Many Indias: Many Literatures*. New Critical Series. Delhi: World View Publications, 2001.

Pirandello, Luigi. *Six Characters in Search of an Author*. "Pirandeflo: Three Plays Trans Author Livingstone. London: J.M. Dent & Sons Ltd., 1922.

Rath, Karthik Chandra. *Bahniman* (Oriya). Cuttack: Jagannath Rath, 1977

Said, Edward. *Orientalism*. Hamondsworth: Penguin, 1985.

Sarma, Arun. "Buranjipat" *Arun Sarmar Nirbachita Natak* (Assamese). Guwahati: Phani Sarma Sumarini Samiti, 2001.

Satchidanandan, K. *Indian Literature: Positions and Propositions*. Delhi: Pencraft International 1999.

Satpathy, Bijay Kumar. *Ei Je Surya Uen* (Oriya). Cuttack: Barnamala Prakashan, 1987.

Schechner, Richard. *Performative Circumstances: From the Advant-Grade to Ramlila*. Calcutta: Seagull Books, 1983.

Selden, Raman. *A Reader's Guide to Contemporary Literary Theory*. Second Edition. London: Harvester Wheatsheaf. 1989.

Sengupta, Sankar and K.D. Upadhyaya. Eds. *Studies in Indian Folk Culture*. Calcutta: Indian Publication, 1964.

Singleton, Brian. "K.N. Panikkar's *Teyyateyyam*: Resisting Interculturalism Through Ritual Practice". *Indian Literature* (205), 133 - 140.

Sircar, Badal. *The Third Theatre*. Calcutta: Badal Sircar, 1983.

_______________ . *Beyond the Land of Hattamala and Scandal in Fairyland*. Trans. from Bengali. Suchanda Sircar. Calcutta: Seagull Books, 1992.

Tagore, Rabindra Nath. *Three Plays*. Trans. from Bengali and with an Introduction, Ananda Lal. New Delhi: Oxford University Press, 2001.

Tanvir, Habib. *Charandas Chor*. Trans. Anjum Katyal. Calcutta: Seagull Books, 1996.

_______________ . "Use of Music and Dance in Contemporary Dramatic Performance". *Theatre Journal* (1961) 1-2:57-59.

Tendulkar, Vijay. *Ghashiram Katwal*. Trans. from Marathi, Jayant Karve and Eleanor Zelliot. Calcutta: Seagull Books, 1986.

Thiyam, Ratan. *Chakravyuha*. Pre–text and Reconstructed Text by Kavita Nagpal. Calcutta: Seagull Books, 1998.

Trivedi, Harish. "India and Post-colonial Discourse". *Critical Theory: Western and Indian*. Ed. Prafulla C. Kar. Delhi: Pencraft International, 1997.

Vatsayan, Kapila. *Traditional Indian Theatre: Multiple Streams*. New Delhi: National Book Trust of India, 1980.

Verma, Surendra. "From Sunset to Sunrise". Trans. from Hindi, Jaya Krishnamachari. *Modern Indian Drama*. Ed. Deshpande.

Viswanathan, Gauri. *Masks of Conquest. Literary Study and British Rule in India*. New York: Columbia University Press, 1989.

Index